THE NEW GOCCO GUIDE

CREATING WITH PRINT GOCCO

Claire Russell

THINK INK

Published by Think Ink
A Division of Creative Enterprises, Inc.
7526 Olympic View Drive, Suite E
Edmonds, Washington 98026-5556
U.S.A.

www.thinkink.net

Material for this book came from the author's research
and experience. The author has made great effort to ensure
that all techniques are accurate and safe, but the author is
not responsible for the failure of any product or technique to
perform as expected.

First edition published 1997
Printed in the United States of America
10 9 8 7 6 5 4 3 2 1

ISBN 0-9655387-0-2

Library of Congress Catalog Card Number 97-91107

Dedicated to our creative spirit,
May we strive and stretch to hear it.

CONTENTS

ACKNOWLEDGMENTS	3
HOW TO USE THIS MANUAL	7
THE GENERAL IDEA	11
GETTING STARTED	15
PREPARING DESIGNS	29
PAPER	41
MULTICOLOR PRINTING	47
EMBOSSING	69
MIXED MEDIA	81
MAXIMIZING MATERIALS	85
PHOTO SCREEN	99
FELT PRINTING	107
REGISTRATION	113
STAMP KIT FOR CLOTH	153
SCREEN KIT PG	179
PROJECTS	199
TROUBLESHOOTING	217
APPENDIX	233

ACKNOWLEDGMENTS

Mary Worthington deserves a special thank you for writing the first GOCCO GUIDE with me. Without her, there would have been neither that book nor this one.

Mary Shirley spent many hours on the illustrations. Look for "MS" on all her efforts. This book would still be unfinished if Mary had not fit this endeavor into her already busy schedule. Anna Axel's reliable and competent help freed time for me to sit at my computer. Jo Forsyth helped with early editing. Shereen LaPlantz inspired me and most generously shared her expertise.

Elizabeth Walsh, creative spirit with good left-brain skills, was a great help in making this an intelligible book and equally generous with motivation to see the project to completion.

My son and business partner, Douglas, was generous with moral support, computer assistance and even flowers!

Travis, my patient husband, showed me that the training regimen to prepare for a bicycle race was no different from that required to write a book. By both word and example he inspired me to persevere. A little gift of chocolate now and then was an extra stimulus!

Thank you, all of you. You sustained me!

Claire Russell

HOW TO USE
THIS MANUAL

HOW TO USE THIS MANUAL

First, review the table of contents and flip through the chapters just to see what's in store for you and your Gocco Printer. If you are new to Gocco Printing, carefully read GETTING STARTED and PREPARING THE ORIGINAL. They will start you on your way to successful and creative projects. If you are a veteran printer, you still may glean a new hint or two from these two chapters. TROUBLESHOOTING will help you through frustrations and problems.

Most of the book is gingerbread…the fun stuff. If you are unsure what to do with a Gocco Printer, the PROJECTS chapter will inspire your with the usefulness and versatility of the Gocco Printers. If you are looking for ideas on specific aspects of printing, check the concluding *possibilities* section of many chapters.

Caution: Gocco Printing can become addictive! Your life can easily be overrun with paper and all your Gocco printed items. This is not a *complete* exaggeration…it does happen!

Have fun! Ah, creativity!

THE GENERAL IDEA

THE GENERAL IDEA

Before getting into details, let's have a brief explanation of what a Gocco Printer is and how it works: The Gocco Printer is a simple, easy, hand-operated printing press. It has multitudinous uses that can inspire creativity in many directions. Artists, crafters, hobbyists, clubs, small businesses, and teachers ranging from pre-school to college, all find the Gocco Printers to be a valuable tool.

The Gocco will print multiple colors at one time on a variety of papers: napkins, bags, envelopes, business cards, stationery, and greeting cards. It can print on cloth, ribbon, mylar, metal, glass, wood, or even your walls!

The Gocco Printers do not replace other printing methods. Lithography, etching, monoprinting, screen printing, commercial printing, etc., all fulfill special needs. The Gocco meets some needs we didn't even know we had! Have you even thought of printing personalized napkins, lunch sacks or stationery? Now that you know you can do these things, and do them so easily, a new world of graphic possibilities opens colorful and exciting doors.

The Gocco Printers are simple to operate. They are in the seeing-is-believing category. Your design is quickly transferred to the Print Master when the flash bulbs go off. One quick flash and that's it! The Master is sensitive to the heat, not the light, of the bulbs. Squeeze ink from a tube on to the exposed Master. A Mylar top sheet covers the Master making a thin ink "sandwich." With each printing, a small amount of the ink is pressed through the exposed portion of the Master onto the printing surface. An inked Master will yield 75 or more copies. The Master can be reinked, making several hundred or more good, quality prints. Masters can be cleaned, stored for later use, and reinked with different colors.

That's it, but that's also just the beginning! Most of this manual deals with the exciting variations on this simple theme.

Here's to your creative spirit, may you strive and stretch to hear it!

GETTING STARTED

PRINT MASTERS

BLUE FILTER

FLASH BULBS

BATTERIES

FOAM BASE

PRINT MASTER: EXPOSING

SAFEGUARDS

PRINT MASTER: INKING

PRINT MASTER: PRINTING

DRYING

NOTEBOOK: IDEA COLLECTING

GETTING STARTED

Understanding how a Gocco Printer works will help you plan your projects and avoid frustration. This is an introduction to the important parts and functioning of the Printer: exposing the Master, inking and printing.

PRINT MASTERS

Print Masters are the essence of Gocco Printers. It is the Print Master that receives the image from your original design, and then the ink for printing.

The light blue side of a Print Master is two materials bonded together: the shiny blue film on the outside is a thin layer of heat-sensitive saran; the inside is woven porous mesh. The outer saran layer is the surface that your original design touches when the bulbs flash.

The carbon black in the original design absorbs heat from the flashing bulbs. The bulbs generate enough heat to melt away the saran where the carbon touches the saran. This exposes the mesh layer of the Master.

Remove exposed Print Master from Printer for inking. Lift up Mylar cover sheet. Squeeze ink out of the tubes onto the inside mesh layer of the Master. Ink will only pass through areas of the Master where the saran film on the outside of the Master has melted away. The clear Mylar top sheet will cover the ink and completes an ink "sandwich."

Replace inked Master in Printer. Place the paper to be printed on the foam base pad. Firmly press down top of Printer, containing inked Master, on to the paper. Enough ink will squeeze out of the Master to leave an ink image of your design on your printing surface.

PUTTING A PRINT MASTER IN THE PRINTER

B6 MASTER

The Master fits into the Printer only one way. The Mylar top sheet of the Master faces the window. The tab with a down-pointing arrow is at the bottom of the Master, offset to the left side. The tab fits into a notch in the bottom bracket that holds the Master. Push Master down firmly. Bow the Master out slightly to slip the top edge of the Master into the top bracket.

B5 MASTER

This Master slides into the brackets horizontally from right to left. Hold Master so arrow on bottom of Master points to the left.

The Master will also slide in upside down with the arrow on the top and pointing to the right. The problem here is that the Mylar sheet is loose on the left side of the Master and can be pushed back when you slide in the Master. Imagine what a mess this could create with an inked Master! (See MAXIMIZING MATERIALS, CLEANING AND STORING PRINT MASTERS p. 89)

B6 and B5 Print Masters fit into Printers

BLUE FILTER

Use the Blue Filter when an original is a photo copy or a laser print. Never use a Filter with *real* originals. The Master will not expose completely and will not print clearly. If an original is a paste-up of several components, photo copies and *real* originals, it may be possible to slide the Filter in part way between Master and Window so the Filter covers only the photo copied area. Otherwise, photo copy the entire design and use the Filter.

With the B6 Printer put the Filter in the Printer first, then put in the Master, so the Filter is sandwiched between the "window" and Print Master. With the B5 Printer, slide in Filter and Master together with Filter facing "window." Just remember—Filter First!

Take care of your Filter and it will last indefinitely. Store Filter in an envelope to keep it clean and unscratched.

B6 and B5 Masters and Filters

FLASH BULBS

A B6 Printer needs two bulbs to expose a Master. A B5 Printer takes 4. Bulbs are used just once, but an exposed Master will yield many prints. To insert bulbs into the Flash Housing, line up the two small knobs on bulb base with notches in Housing sockets. Push bulb down and give it half a turn.

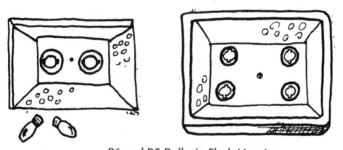

B6 and B5 Bulbs in Flash Housing

TYPES OF BULBS

Bulbs that come with the Printer are different from regular flash bulbs. Gocco bulbs are made to produce heat. It is heat, not light that exposes a Master. Photographic flash bulbs are made for light. Photographic bulbs generally produce a Master that is not thoroughly exposed. Signs of an underexposed Master are lines and areas that do not print solidly.

BATTERIES

Bulbs do not go off spontaneously! It takes battery power to make flash bulbs go off. This sounds simplistic, but more than one person has not known there were batteries "hidden" inside the Printer!

B6 PRINTERS

Printer includes two AA batteries. The battery compartment is in the underside of the Printer handle. Push up on the two squares marked "Push" to slide up the panel on the bottom side of the handle. Put in batteries noting the +/- terminals. Replace panel.

B5 PRINTERS

Printers come with three C batteries already in position. The battery compartment is on top of Printer along hinge side of window. Remove the tab of white paper sticking out from the compartment to activate the batteries.

 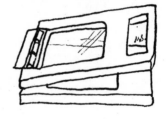

Batteries in B6 Printer   Batteries in B5 Printer

FOAM BASE

Printers have a tacky base on the Foam Pad. Remove protective plastic sheet from tacky base of a new Printer... fingernails help. The base is just tacky enough to hold paper on it after printing rather than having the paper stick to the Master. This gives a clean release of paper from the Master and prevents smudging. The Base will hold grid paper to help in registration. (See REGISTRATION, p. 113)

PRINT MASTER: EXPOSING

- Put a piece of plain white paper on the Foam Base. Place original design face up and straight on white paper. It is hard to print straight if design is placed crooked on the Master. (The design will adhere to the Master after flashing.)

- Remember to use Blue Filter if design is a photo copy. Place filter between "window" of Printer and Print Master.

- Check to be sure Master is in Printer.

- Lower Printer top over original and see how everything looks. Make sure design is not too close to cardboard frame of Master.

FLASH TO EXPOSE

Ready? Let's take this step-by-step:

- Place Flash Housing over window. Line up small arrow on Flash Housing with arrow on Printer.

- Place back of B6 Flash Housing (nearest to the hinge) down into Printer first, then front part.

- On the B5 Printer the arrows are on the *front*, facing you.

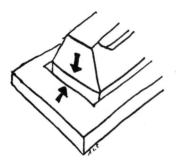

Arrow on back of B6 Flash Housing lining up with arrow on Printer & arrows on front of B-5 Printer and Flash Housing

- Push down top of Printer firmly to close contacts— FLASH! That's it.

- Remove Housing, checking that all the bulbs flashed. It is rare for a bulb to fail, but if this happens, put in all new bulbs and flash again.
- Lift up the Printer lid, remover Master, put Filter away and discard bulbs when cool.

The exposed Master will yield many prints. It can be cleaned, saved, reinked later with different colors. Unlike silk screens which can be reused for different designs, the image burned into a Master is permanent.

SAFEGUARDS

The newer models of both printers, blue B6 and gray B5, have safeguard buttons so bulbs will not flash unless a Master is in place. Older orange and yellow B6 Printers and yellow B5 Printers do not have this feature.

B6 PRINTERS

The Master pushes the orange tab out of the "window" opening so the Flash Housing will drop down to meet the battery contacts.

Older yellow and even older orange models of B6 Printers do not have this safeguard. You must remember to put in a Master before flashing the bulbs. Forget and you will ruin the plastic *window*. The design will be etched into the plastic. (A quick way to etch plastic, but....)

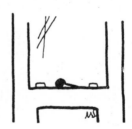

Orange safety button on B6 Printer

If you put in the Filter but forgot the Master, the photo copy toner will adhere permanently to the Filter. You will need a new Filter, because toner on the Filter will transfer to . the next Master.

B5 PRINTERS

On the Gray B5 there is a small, silvery button at the left end of the top bracket that holds the Master. Be sure to slide Master to the left until button is depressed, otherwise the bulbs will not flash. This button also prevents sliding a Master in the bracket from the left rather than the right side.

Safety Button on B5 Gocco

IS THIS REALLY NECESSARY?

All this may sound silly...How could anyone forget to put in the Master? The Master is essential to the whole process. Just remember, in the heat of creativity, details, even critical ones, get lost!

PRINT MASTER: INKING

Before inking the Master, gently peel back part of the original design and look carefully at the Master just to be sure everything is O.K. (See TROUBLESHOOTING, INSPECT EXPOSED MASTER, p. 220.) Don't remove the original completely. It is easier to ink the Master if the original is still attached to it, as a guide.

Place Master on a table, Mylar side up. Lift up Mylar top sheet, fold it back. Select ink colors. Squeeze out a bead of ink about $1/8''$ thick, tracing along lines of writing or zigzag across solid areas. Smooth out ink with a spatula.

Ink amounts vary with copy density, the desired number of prints, and paper absorbency. For example, a line of typing with an $1/8''$ bead of ink will print about 100 copies, often more, but large solid areas will require more ink. If you ink the Master too generously, excess ink will ooze out the sides of Master creating a mess!

Replace the Mylar cover sheet. You now have an ink sandwich. Remove original from Master. Some ink may have gone through Master on to your original—a good reason not to use your only original to make a Master.

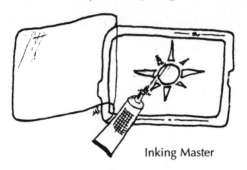

Inking Master

PRINT MASTER: PRINTING

B6 PRINTER
After inking Master, place Master in the Printer the same way you did when you exposed the Master.

B5 PRINTER
The B5 Printer comes with a Cushion Sheet that helps ink to print evenly.

- Place Cushion Sheet next to inked Master, foam side of Cushion next to Mylar side of Master.

- Slide Cushion Sheet and Master together into brackets that hold Master.

- The Cushion Sheet will be next to the glass window of the printer.

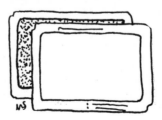

B5 Cushion Sheet

PAPER PLACEMENT IN B5 PRINTER

GUIDE BAR

The Guide Bar is along the back side of the Foam Base. Adjust guides for different sizes of paper. The guides can hold about 20 sheets of light weight paper for printing.

- Lift up Guide Bar, place paper on Base. Lower Guides on top of paper and adjust to width of paper. Tighten small white knobs on Guide Bar to secure guide corners.

- Paper to a maximum of 13.9" (B4 size) can be held in guides by attaching extenders at ends of Guide Bar. (Extenders are included with Printer.) Paper will rest on *top* of these guides.

- Pull Guide Bar forward and back, about 3/4", by adjusting the larger white knobs near hinges of Printer.

Guide Bar on B5 Printer

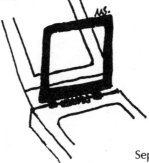

Separator on B5 Printer

SEPARATOR

Snap Separator, which was removed to expose Master, onto hinge rod at back of Printer. Separator will pull printed paper from Master as top of Printer is raised up.

Note: The Separator only works on large sheets of paper.

PAPER

Put a piece of test paper on Foam Base, lower Printer, press down until lid meets resistance of Foam Base. Lift up lid. Remove print, put in another paper, make a couple more prints, then go to your good paper.

EXPERIMENT

Once Master is inked, it's easy to experiment: See how the same design looks on napkins, lunch bags, post cards, various colors and types of papers. Change placement of the printed image: the bottom, side or top of the paper, at an angle, or repeat the image. (See REGISTRATION, PAPER PLACEMENT, p. 114, for alignment techniques.)

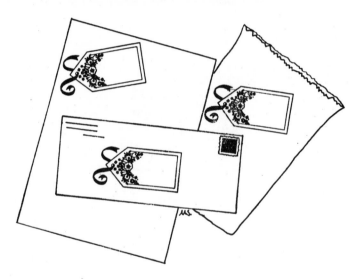

Samples of Placement of same design in various items

REINKING THE MASTER

Watch prints for areas that haven't printed, a sign that ink is running out. Remove Print Master from Printer. Lift up Mylar top sheet, and hold Master up to the light. You will see light shining through areas that need reinking.

Place the Master on a scrap of paper, Mylar side up to add ink as needed. For just a few more copies you may not have to add ink. Try smoothing ink around enough to cover the bare spots, and finish printing.

DRYING

Drying time depends on the paper: Paper napkins dry quickly, about 10 minutes. Glossy coated papers take longer. Fine lines dry faster than larger solid areas.

Drying takes not only time, but space. Keep printing and soon you will surround yourself with paper, the Gocco equivalent of painting yourself into a corner! Here are some ways to handle the results of your Gocco exuberance:

GOCCO CARD RACKS

2/pkg. Each rack is $2^3/_4''$ x $8^3/_4''$ and holds 20 cards. Card Racks, true to their names, are for cards; larger sheets of light weight paper flop over.

Gocco Card Rack

SLINKY

Remember this coiled toy? Stretch it out and use as a long drying rack. This, too, works best with cards.

TRAYS COOKIE SHEETS

Use these for napkins and large sheets of paper. Stack several trays or cookie sheets next to your Printer. (Now that you are discovering Gocco-printing, you won't have time to bake cookies anyway!) Place printed items on top tray, when it is full, put tray aside to dry. Stack trays with edges in a staggered manner.

NOTEBOOK: IDEA COLLECTING

Get a ring binder and a glue stick. Put in some blank sheets of paper. Store your new book near your Printer so it's easy to add in your latest creations. Keep a record of color combinations, papers, etc. Make notes of what worked and what did not. Collect ideas for future projects. You will impress yourself, not to mention your family, friends, and clients.

PREPARING DESIGNS

IMAGE AREA: SIZE

CARBON BLACK

OTHER MATERIALS WITH CARBON

NON-CARBON BLACK

OTHER CAUTIONS

GENERAL ADVICE

PREPARING DESIGNS

The most important aspect of using a Print Gocco is preparation of the original design used to expose a Print Master. Gocco Printers are easy to operate, but the finished product will be no better than what you begin with.

SIZE OF IMAGE AREA

- B-6 Printer: Maximum size of original is 4″ x 5 $^3/_4$″
- B-5 Printer: Maximum size is 6″ x 9″

It is important that your design be no larger that these sizes even though there is space for a larger design on the Master. Larger designs or designs placed close to the frame around the Master will not expose well near the frame. Note: These dimensions are slightly larger than the conservative ones given in the Gocco Printer specifications.

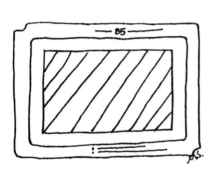 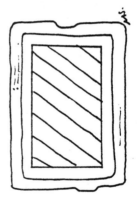

Note image area of B-5 and B-6 Masters

CARBON BLACK

Original design used to expose the Master must be a *carbon* black. It is the carbon in the black that absorbs the heat from the flash bulbs and in turn melts away the portion of the Master that is touching the design. Just because an ink or pen *looks* black does not mean that it contains carbon. The black may be from dye rather than from carbon. The lists that follow are only beginnings to get you started.

CARBON INKS

Ink bottles do not list the composition of ink, so it is not obvious which inks contain carbon. These are some brands of ink, often used for calligraphy and drafting, which are carbon-based.

- Calli Water Proof Pigment Ink
- Higgins Black Magic Ink
- Higgins Eternal, #813
- Higgins Non-Waterproof India Ink #4425
- Higgins Fountain Pen India, #723 by Faber Castell Corp.
- Kohinoor
- Pelikan Fount India
- Pelikan Drawing Ink
- Pelikan Special Black Drawing Ink #50
- Penelack, made by Boku Undo
- Sumi inks and stick inks (Sumi inks are "liquid versions" of stick inks.)
- Technical pen inks, e.g., Reform, Rapidograph, Staedtler Mars, and Kohinoor

CARBON PAINTS

Several artists paints contain carbon. These are a few; there are probably more.

- Golden Acrylic black
- Winsor & Newton Lamp Black gouache
- Winsor & Newton Lamp Black water color

CARBON PENS

RISO PENS

A fine point carbon pen is included with the B6, and 3 different pens are included with the B5 Printer. There are several double end carbon pens made by the Riso Company, manufacturers of the Gocco Printers, to use specifically with the Gocco Printer.

• Fine .1/.5

•Fine .3/.8

•Fine/Medium

•Medium/Bold

•Calligraphy/Bold

•Brush fine/Brush bold

OTHER CARBON PENS

Some of these pens come in colors, but only the black ones contain carbon. This list is only a sampling.

- Pentel Hybrid K105
- Pigma Micro Perma Roller
- Pigma Micron
- Sakura Gelly Roll, XPGB, black

- Sakura Pigma Graphic
- Technical pens, e.g., Reform and Kohinoor, (see inks)
- Zig Calligraphy Extra, Water-proof Pigment Ink

PENCILS

Pencil sketches can make a very nice Gocco print, but take care which pencil you use. Hard lead, which makes a lighter line, will not work well. Softer leads, ebony and charcoal pencils will expose a Master well.

A few notes of caution:

- Do not make any pencil guide lines on your design that you do not want to expose.
- Be careful to shake any pencil dust off your artwork before exposing Master.
- Results will vary depending on how dark a line you make.

BLACK CRAYON

Black crayon will expose the Master. Draw the original on rough paper, print on the same type of rough paper and the print will look very much like an original. Black China Markers, similar to crayon but in a plastic holder, also contain carbon.

Black crayon on rough paper

BLACK PAPER

Experiment with torn paper for a collage effect. Many black papers have carbon, including carbon typing paper.

- Canson Mi-Teintes paper produces two effects: One side is smooth and exposes the Master evenly. The other side has just a slight texture and exposes the master with an irregular dotted pattern.

- Large areas of black may have small unexposed spots...see TROUBLESHOOTING, EXPOSING LARGE SOLID AREAS, p. 222.

OTHER MATERIALS WITH CARBON

PHOTO COPIES

The instructions that come with the Printer recommend using a PPC photo copy machine, i.e., plain paper copier. Almost all copiers now use plain paper.

The toner in black photo copies contains carbon, but it is a concentrated carbon much denser than the carbon in any of the inks or pens mentioned here. Set the copy machine on medium or light, just dark enough not to loose the fine lines and details. Even when set on light, photo copies tend to have too much toner. To compensate, always use the Blue Filter when exposing a photo copy.

The quality of copy machines varies; use one that gives clear, crisp results. An individual copier will also vary depending on when it has been serviced. (See TROUBLESHOOTING, p. 217. for more details on photo copies.)

COMPUTER OUTPUT

Laser Printers have carbon in the toner cartridges they use. Laser prints vary by brand, adjustment, and how much the cartridge has been used. With a new cartridge, you may need to use the Blue Filter. With an older cartridge, the Master may not expose well if you use the Filter. This, obviously, will require some experimenting.

Ink jet printers do not contain toner in their ink. Dot matrix printers generally will not work unless the ribbon is new.

TYPING

- Typing done with a Mylar ribbon, not a cloth ribbon, contains carbon. Do a test with your ribbon to be sure.

- Carbon copies also have carbon, but they may not be clear. New carbon paper is best.

COMMERCIALLY PRINTED ITEMS

- Commercial printing done with black ink, e.g., the clip art included with the Printer.
- Newspaper printing works, but the images are not very clean and apt to produce pin dots.
- Photo copy the newspaper clipping first.

BLACK RUBBER STAMPED IMAGES

Use a well-inked pigmented stamp pad. The stamped image should be crisp. Color Box black pads are particularly good.

NON-CARBON BLACK

Avoid designs made with any of these non-carbon materials. They will *not* work! They may *look* like a carbon black, but they do not *act* like carbon, because the black is a dye rather than carbon.

DYE INKS

- Script
- Panache Fountain Pen Ink
- Parker Super Quink Ink
- Pelikan 4001
- Sheaffer, including Sheaffer ink cartridges.

    Note: Refill empty cartridges with carbon ink.

DYE PENS

ROLLING BALL TYPE PENS
There are many. These are two common ones:

- Stylist Super
- Pilot V Ball
- Pilot Razor Point

FELT AND FIBER TIP PENS

Most felt type markers do not contain carbon.

- Speedball Elegant Writer
- Fiber "Brush" pens such as the Staedtler Mars Graphic 3000 Duo
- Tombow ABT, contains some carbon, but not enough to expose well.

BRUSH PENS

Pentel Black Brush Pen contains some carbon. It will work for a dry brush look only.

OTHER NON-CARBONS

Colored photo copies or black photo copies made on a color copier.

- Photographs, even black and white ones, contain silver, not carbon.
- Photostats and Veloxes: these are photographic products and generally do not contain carbon. Also, they have a slight gloss.

OTHER CAUTIONS

These are details that are easy to overlook, but they can affect the quality of your work.

PAPER FOR YOUR ORIGINAL

Use smooth white non glossy paper to draw your design. Twenty pound white bond paper is fine, often sold as copier or laser paper. Avoid textured paper, unless you *want* a rough irregular effect, e.g., drawing with black crayon on cold press water color paper.

GOCCO PENS

Even though these pens contain carbon, they can cause problems. The ink needs to be very dry before it will expose the Master. Dry to the touch is not enough. When filling in a large solid area, the ink dries slowly. Hasten drying with a hair dryer or allow a few hours.

SHINY SURFACES

Some materials, even though they contain carbon, will not work because they are shiny. Dull surfaces absorb heat and shiny surfaces reflect heat. Even a slight sheen will make a poorly exposed Master.

- Photo copy all shiny surfaces, but check your photo copy! Photo copies may also be shiny, especially those with large solid areas. A copy machine may produce satisfactory copies of line art, but on larger areas it may produce a slight sheen. Avoid these copies. Setting the machine on light probably will not help. Try another copier.

- Glossy or semi-glossy paper used in magazines and many clip art books.

- Some inks are shiny. Pelikan Fount India Ink, Penelack, and Sumi inks, if applied thickly, will dry with a slight sheen. Try Higgins Fountain Pen India. It dries to a matte finish.

- The Gocco pens may make the surface shiny when used to fill in a large area.

- Pencil filled in areas may become shiny.

- Scotch tape…don't use it over your original.

- Art work done on glossy paper, including onion skin and tracing paper.

WHITE OUT and LIQUID PAPER

Use with care in covering up goofs on your original. The White Out may cover up the error visually, but the Gocco may still "see" the carbon under the White Out and print some of it. Don't write over White Out. The Master will not expose this area well. If you have made many corrections, photo copy your design.

Another caution in using White Out is that it tends to dry thick and raised on the paper. Just this little thickness will lift the Master up from the paper and prevent the Master from exposing thoroughly.

NON-PHOTO BLUE PENCILS AND NON-PHOTO BLUE GRID PAPER

Most non-photo blues do not contain carbon, but some, even though they are blue, not black, will copy on the Master. Test yours first. You don't want a Master with a grid pattern superimposed on it.

LINES

Make clear solid lines. Look closely at fine lines to make sure they are solid and not dotted. Do not press down so hard when writing that the lines indent into the paper. The lines that are in the "valleys" will not touch the Master, and will not expose the Master.

PASTE UPS

Be careful when pasting several elements together to complete your design. The small steps created by the layers of paper can prevent the Master from being completely exposed. The original needs to be *touching* the Master, not just "looking" at it in order to expose the Master. Keep paper overlaps at least 1/2" away from an image. Trim paper so edges meet evenly, end to end, instead of overlapping.

Use small dabs of glue stick to secure pieces of paper. Avoid a wet glue such as Elmer's. Use Scotch tape carefully. Do not cover any part of the design and keep tape at least 1/2" away from image.

DIRT

Store Masters in their package until ready to use. Keep your art work clean of eraser crumbs, pencil dust, smudges, dirty finger prints, smeared glue, etc. Cleanliness is important…didn't your mother tell you the same thing?

HEAT

Store Masters in a cool place. (The *heat* of flash bulbs exposes Masters.) Excessive heat may damage them, including a car on a hot day.

GENERAL ADVICE

LOOK BEFORE YOU FLASH

It is easy to give your design a cursory glance and see in your mind's eye what it will become, already perceiving it as the finished product. Get in the habit of *carefully* looking over your original before you expose the Master. You will be glad later for your attention to these details.

WHEN IN DOUBT, DO A TEST

- Use an empty part of the Master next time you are exposing a design. You can experiment with unknowns this way without ruining a whole Master.

- If you have numerous things to test, use one Master to make all your tests.

- Keep your test results in your Gocco notebook for reference. We hate to admit it, but sometime we do forget important details!

COPY YOUR ORIGINAL

Don't use your original to expose a Master if it is something you want to save. Some of the carbon from the original may adhere to the Master, or you may get ink on it when you are inking the Master.

Gocco instructions advise against using an original more than once to expose a Master. In practice, an original will expose more than one Master.

PAPER

SUITABLE PAPERS

SOME SUGGESTIONS

CONSIDERATIONS

OTHER SURFACES

WHERE TO LOOK

PAPER

Paper and Gocco printing are synonymous. New Gocco owners quickly print on every "unattached" piece of paper and soon are on the prowl for more.

SUITABLE PAPERS

One of the benefits of Gocco printing is the wide range of papers suitable for printing. Ordinary white paper comes to mind first, but it's a small step to paper napkins, lunch sacks, Kleenex, tissue paper and even toilet paper! Business cards, envelopes, stationery, and wrapping paper may appeal to you more than toilet paper, but all are good printing surfaces. Even very shiny Krome Kote can be used.

Text weight paper, a medium-light weight paper, is good for stationery, and handmade books; card stock is good for greeting cards. Smooth finish papers are best to show fine details, but rough, handmade paper adds a nice texture for some projects.

Note, when printing on very rough paper, ink will not get down into the "valleys" of the paper. In addition ink will build up on the Master over these valleys. This ink build up will leave globs of ink on your next print. The remedy is to print a scrap sheet after each print to remove the build up from the Master.

Make your own colorful stickers by printing on pressure sensitive blank stickers. Avery is a common brand of vari-colored and shaped stickers.

SOME SUGGESTIONS

COMMERCIAL PAPERS

"Commercial papers" refers to paper sold by the ream or box and cut to smaller sizes than art papers. If you are printing 100 or more cards or sheets of stationery, this is probably what you want.

- Look for $8\,^1/_2''$ x 11" or $8\,^1/_2''$ x 14" text or cover weight paper. Often there are matching envelopes in A-2, A-6, A-7 and #10 sizes.

- Greeting card stores sell envelopes and paper by the sheet, an expensive way to purchase paper, but fine if you need a small amount for a special project. Some of these papers have pre-printed borders that are perfect for Gocco printing an invitation or poem.

ART PAPERS

"Art papers" are often large, parent size, sheets of paper that you can cut, or fold and tear to a more manageable size. Look for papers made for printmaking. Papers for printmaking and silk-screen printing are receptive to printing inks, including Gocco ink. The following list is but a sampler of ideas.

PRINTMAKING PAPER

- Arches 88 and Magnani Pescia (Incisioni), are printmaking papers.

- Oriental block printing papers such as Hosho Professional will take a Gocco print well.

- If you want colored paper, check Canson Mi-Teintes paper, which come in many colors.

OTHER PAPERS

Try many papers. Some of the most unlikely ones will be wonderful!

- Silk Span is an inexpensive, strong, sheer, almost transparent, paper that can be Gocco printed for an interesting effect. It can even be embossed.

- Clear Mylar can be Gocco printed and used for a greeting card overlay.

- Print on silvery Mylar, or use it as a "mirror" in a card.

- Rough texture paper compliments bold/rough Gocco-printed designs. Use smoother hot press water color paper for more even results and fine details.

- There are many decorative oriental papers. Print on lace papers. Use them for overlays and as end papers for Gocco-printed books. Some papers have small flecks of gold and silver imbedded in the paper. Print on these with metallic inks.

CAUTION

If in doubt, look for a paper made for printmaking or for commercial printing. Some wonderful papers are not made for printing. Their surface is not receptive to ink, and Gocco ink will not adhere well to such a surface.

MORE INFORMATION

Consult Shereen LaPlantz's informative book, DESIGNING AND WORKING WITH GOCCO for much useful information on printing on many types of paper, (see APPENDIX, p. 234).

CONSIDERATIONS

For a project requiring envelopes, select envelopes first. The available sizes and colors of envelopes is more limited than the choice of papers.

When cutting large sizes of paper, you'll need a straight edge and a sharp X-Acto or snap off blade knife. Smaller paper will fit in a paper cutter. Banish your scissors for making straight cuts! For large jobs, your paper supplier or local printer will cut your paper for a nominal charge.

OTHER SURFACES

You are limited only by the scope of your imagination! If in doubt, *try printing on it!* The worst that can happen is that it will not work. There are many non-paper surfaces awaiting you:

- Tyvek is a very strong, white synthetic paper. It can be colored with acrylic inks and takes Gocco ink nicely. Tyvek also comes with a softer cloth-like feel for wind breakers and disposable garments. This has many possibilities for promotional and fun jackets. You may have noticed that Tyvek is also used as an insulation material in the home building industry.

- Ultra Suede, leather, feathers, leaves, disposable baby diapers, and wood are but a few surfaces to try. See PROJECTS, p. 199 for more ideas.

WHERE TO LOOK

- Check you local printer. Often print shops give away end cuts that are odd sizes of paper left from their printing jobs. These assorted shapes, sizes, and colors of paper may be just perfect for Gocco printing. The paper itself may inspire a project: narrow strips of paper make perfect book markers. Weave narrow strips of paper to make a place mat and print on it.

- Salvage stores may be a source for surplus or discontinued paper and envelopes.

- Check the Yellow Pages for paper suppliers, stationery and art stores. Some paper companies have a surplus table for cash-and-carry customers.

- Art supply stores stock a wide array of papers.

- See APPENDIX, OTHER SUPPLIES, p. 240.

Print on other surfaces: feathers, leaves

MULTICOLOR PRINTING

"IN LIVING COLOR!"

THE GOCCO PALETTE

MIXING COLORS

A BIT OF COLOR THEORY

CREATING NEW COLORS

INK BLOCK

ADJOINING COLORS

REINKING A MULTICOLOR MASTER

POSSIBILITIES

MULTICOLOR PRINTING

"IN LIVING COLOR!"

Color and Gocco printing are almost synonymous. The ability to print many colors in just one inking is one of the most appealing features of Gocco Printing. Newcomers to Gocco printing always show a delightful look of surprise when they see their first multicolor-color Gocco print. The cost of one multicolor-color job done at a commercial print shop could pay for a Gocco Printer, even a large B5 model.

THE GOCCO PALETTE

There are several categories of Gocco ink colors. These lists will be a handy reference before we start mixing more colors.

Meet the cast of characters. There are no "supporting roles"... they are all unique!

BASIC COLORS

These are the colors which are included with both the B5 and B6 Printers

- Black
- Brown
- White
- Red
- Blue
- Green
- Yellow

PASTEL COLORS

- Blue
- Green
- Lavender
- Light Orange
- Pink

METALLIC COLORS
The Metallics are truly metallic, not just metallic-colored. The Metallics and Pearls have the same shimmery base.

- Bronze
- Gold
- Silver

PEARLESCENT COLORS
The Pearls are a bit darker than the Pastels.

- Blue
- Green
- Red
  Note: Pearl Red is closer to rose, not red.

FLUORESCENT COLORS
These are bright eye-popping colors. But wait a minute before you dismiss them, thinking they are not your "type!" Even if you do not like unadulterated brightness, you will find the Fluorescents very handy for mixing with other colors. You can achieve colors that you just can not mix any other way.

- Green
- Magenta
- Orange
- Pink

PROCESS COLORS
Use these for process color printing or just as great colors on their own.

- Cyan
- Magenta
- Yellow

TRADITIONAL JAPANESE COLORS
These are intense, rich, vibrant colors.

- Burgundy
- Dark Blue
- Dark Brown

- Red-Orange
- Teal
- Yellow-Green

TRANSLUCENT

These new light-color inks are sheer and translucent. They are less opaque than any of the other Gocco inks, including the Pastel Inks. They will not cover other colors or dark papers. They produce a subtle, translucent effect.

They are wonderful for layering colors in multiple printings. The effect looks a bit similar to painting with water color washes in that the first layer of color shows clearly through the second layer.

Note: these are not water-based inks!

- Apple Green
- Baby Blue
- Camel Tan
- Lemon Yellow
- Moon Gray
- Shell Pink

CLOTH INKS

Cloth Inks are water-based inks. They will not mix with the other inks, and are intended just for fabric. They will run and bleed until they are heat set. Once heat-set, they are very washable.

- Black
- Brown
- White
- Red
- Blue
- Green
- Yellow

MIXING COLORS

With visions of splendid rainbows flowing from your Gocco Printer, let's consider the mechanics of mixing inks and getting the mixed ink on the Master. Like anything else, this is easier with the right equipment.

PAPER PALETTES

A tablet of disposable paper palettes from an art supply store is convenient. Mix colors on the palette and discard the top sheet when done.

INK CONES

When using a palette knife or spatula, it is difficult, nearly impossible, to place ink you have mixed precisely on the Master. Ink cones, similar to cake decorating cones, allow you to control the placement and amount of ink on the Master, or improvise using small plastic bags for ink cones.

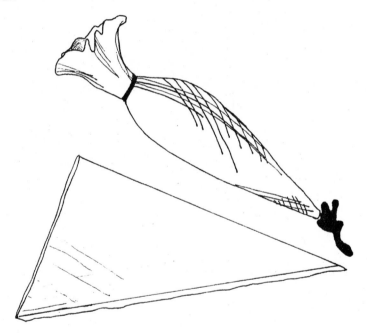

Ink Cones

- Snip off the pointed end of the cone to allow just the right size bead of ink to squeeze out.
- Put ink in the wide open end of the cone. Place cone on a flat surface and run a spatula along the

cone from wide to narrow end, pushing ink down to the tip.

- Fold over the wide end of the cone, and squeeze gently to apply ink to Master. It will be easy to control the amount and placement of ink.
- Use the spatula again to push the last bit of ink from cone.
- Use Ziploc or sandwich bags. Fold the bag in half diagonally across one corner to make the corner into a 45° angle.
- Seal-A-Meal, the gadget used to seal plastic bags for food storage, works to make a diagonal seal across the corner of a bag. Cut away the extra part of the bag.

SPATULAS
Small, flexible spatulas and palette knives work well. Avoid sharp corners or edges that may damage the Master.

- Cut old credit cards to various widths. Round off sharp corners.
- Strips of mat board make fine temporary spatulas.

A BIT OF COLOR THEORY
When you start mixing your own colors, your palette will become vast. Buy a color wheel at an art supply store so you can see how colors relate to each other. Here are some basics on color theory:

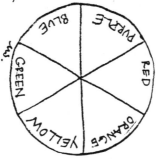

Color Wheel

TINTS

Tints are pastels made by adding a color to white: pink, gray, tan. Start by adding a small amount of color to white. It doesn't take much red to turn white into pink, so begin carefully. Mixing the other way around, adding white to red, may give you enough to paint a barn!

The pastels that you mix are different from the tubes of pastel Gocco Inks. Mix some pastels and you will see these nuances.

Mix a tiny dab of any Fluorescent color with white and get a delicate pastel that does not look fluorescent.

SHADES

Shades are muted, darker colors made by adding black to a color. Black added to pink makes dusty mauve, black added to yellow makes bronze avocado. Begin by adding only tiny amounts of black to a color.

COMPLEMENTS

Complementary colors are directly opposite each other on a color wheel: red-green, blue-orange, purple-yellow. Use complements for strong contrasts and vibrant combinations.

Adding a complement to a color will mute the color. A dot of green added to red will tone down the red, but will not dull it the way black will. Make two swatches of red, one with black added to it and another with green added to it to see the difference. Do the same with the other complements.

Each pair of complements mixed together will make a different hue of brown-gray. These neutrals can add depth and variety to your work. Add to white to make a wide range of taupe, gray and tan tints.

LIMITATIONS OF A COLOR WHEEL

Color wheels are based on a perfect world using pure pigments, but in reality there is no such perfection, neither in pigments nor in the world! Most colors are made with pigments that have traces of other colors in them. Mixing these impure colors distorts the result. Most frustrating is mixing red and blue to make purple. With the Gocco inks, it is a case of "you can't get there from here." Gocco red and blue make a dark dull mauve-purple. Following are directions on how to get to purple and a rainbow of other colors.

CREATING NEW COLORS

EXPERIMENT

Don't underestimate experimentation to learn about colors. Allow time to play with the colors. Mix small amounts on a paper palette or a piece of plain white paper. Fluorescent colors straight from the tube may be too piercing for you, but you can see from the following color list that fluorescent colors are invaluable for mixing other colors.

When you clean your Masters, experiment by mixing the colors you scrape off the Master. You'll learn a lot first hand. Observe the world around you: flowers, current fashions, home decor, even catalogues are full of interesting combinations of colors.

Disposable artist paper palettes are handy. Use a palette knife or an old credit card cut in half lengthwise. (Round off the sharp edges.)

GOCCO INK MIXING

Make these colors with the Gocco tube inks using a palette and spatula. Mix thoroughly to blend the colors. Start with a very small amount of ink to get the exact color you want. Increase the quantity, keeping the same proportions to make enough for your project.

These are only suggestions; vary the proportions and try other combinations. At the very worst, you will make some "yucky" colors and ruin just a dab of ink; but at the best you will have a dazzling rainbow of colors! Remember to start with the lighter color and gradually add the darker color.

PURPLE:
  Mix Blue and Fluorescent Pink
  Blue and Magenta ink

ROYAL BLUE:
  Blue and a bit of Fluorescent Pink

NAVY BLUE:
  Blue and a small amount of Red and a bit of Black

COUNTRY BLUE:
Blue and a bit of Red and White

LAVENDER:
A bit of Fluorescent Magenta and White
Pastel Blue and Fluorescent Pink
Pearl Blue and Fluorescent Pink

MAUVE:
White and small dots of Red and Blue
Magenta and Gray
Lavender and Gray
Pastel Pink and Pastel Blue
Pink and a smidgen of Black

PRUSSIAN BLUE:
Blue with a bit of Fluorescent Orange

TEAL:
Blue and Fluorescent Green

TURQUOISE:
Blue, Fluorescent Green, and White

PALE BLUE GREEN:
Pastel Blue and Pastel Green

BRIGHT GREEN:
Green and Fluorescent Green

FOREST GREEN:
Green and some Brown
Green and a dot of Black
Green and a dot of Red

LIME:
Green and Yellow
Yellow and Fluorescent Green

LIGHT BRIGHT GREEN:
White and a bit of Fluorescent Green

AVOCADO:
Yellow and a tiny dot of Black

ORANGE:
Yellow and Red
Note: This mixture makes a different orange from
Fluorescent Orange, and also blends better in a
rainbow than Fluorescent Orange.

HOT PINK:
Fluorescent Pink and Fluorescent Orange
Fluorescent Pink and Yellow
Fluorescent Pink and Pastel Pink

VERMILION:
Red and Fluorescent Orange

RASPBERRY:
Red and Fluorescent Purple…luscious!

RASPBERRY SHERBET:
Red, Fluorescent Purple, White

BRICK RED:
Brown and Red
Red and a dot of Black

BURGUNDY:
Red a bit of Black and Blue

BROWN:
Fluorescent Orange and Green

TAUPE:
White and a bit of Black and Brown
White and a small amount of complementary colors:
Red & Green; Blue & Orange; Yellow & Purple

RUST:
Fluorescent Orange and Brown

TERRA COTTA:
Fluorescent Orange, a bit of Blue
Fluorescent Orange and Pastel Green
Red, Brown, White
Brown, Pastel Orange
Brown, Fluorescent Orange, White
Pastel Orange and Pastel Blue

PEACH, CORAL, SALMON:
White and Pastel Orange
White and Fluorescent Orange
Pink and a dab of Fluorescent Orange
Pink and Pastel Orange
Pastel Orange and Red
Fluorescent Pink and Yellow
Fluorescent Pink and Fluorescent Orange

PASTEL ORANGE:
Note: The tube of Pastel Orange is the same as White and Fluorescent Orange. Peach mixed from Yellow and Red added to White makes a different color from this Pastel Orange.

PEARL AND METALLIC INKS

If you want to retain the luster of Pearl and Metallic inks, mix only within this group or add just a small amount of the other colors.

These are pretty printed on black paper. They dry to a nice luminous sheen. Be careful printing with pearl or metallic inks and regular inks on dark paper. The two types of ink look quite different, especially if they are used together on one design.

PEARL ROSE:
Pearl Red could more accurately be called "Pearl Rose"

ICY PEARLS:
Mix Pearl Red, Blue or Green with Silver

WARM GOLD:
Gold and Pearl Red
Gold and Bronze

ROSE GOLD:
Gold and Red or Brown

COOL GOLD:
Gold and a bit of Silver

WARMER SILVER:
Silver and a bit of Gold

AQUA:
Pearl Blue and Pearl Green

PEARL MAUVE:
Pearl Blue and Pearl Red

RUST:
Pearl Bronze and Brown

GRAPHITE:
Pearl Silver and a little Black

TRANSLUCENT INKS

These inks will retain their sheer qualities if mixed only within their own group. Try adding just a dab of the more opaque inks to make other colors. These are only a few suggestions:

PEACH:
Lemon Yellow and Shell Pink

TAUPE:
Camel Tan and Mood Gray

AQUA:
Baby Blue and Apple Green

MAUVE:
Shell Pink and Baby Blue

ROSE:
Shell Pink and a dot of Fluorescent Magenta

LAVENDER:
Baby Blue and a dot of Fluorescent Magenta

MUTED COLORS:
Add a dab of Moon Gray to any color

TRADITIONAL COLORS

The intensity of these colors will all make nice pastels if you add just a smidgen of color to white ink. Try this with every one of the six Traditional Colors...you will not be disappointed! These pastels will be different from the regular pastels.

PROCESS INK COLORS

These inks are blended specifically to duplicate four color process printing used by commercial printers, referred to as CMYK colors: cyan (blue), magenta, yellow and black. Process inks are sold in a set of three colors: Cyan, Magenta, and Yellow... you provide the Black.

In four color process printing a multicolor design is separated photographically into four different components producing a separate image for each of the four colors. Starting with a picture of a vase of flowers there will be four images, one showing just the Cyan in the picture, another just the Magenta, etc. The images are dotted patterns. Each color is printed separately, starting with cyan. The magenta component is printed over the cyan, next yellow, then black.

The colored dots superimposed on each other are perceived by our eyes as a rainbow of colors. The resulting print will look like the original. Looking at a process color print with a magnifying glass will show the separate colors.

PREPARING A DESIGN FOR PROCESS PRINTING

There are three ways to have a design prepared for process printing with your Gocco. In all cases a Master is exposed for each of the three colors. See REGISTRATION, PROCESS COLOR PRINTING, p. 148.

- There is a Gocco process color design book which contains many designs which have been separated into the three colors, cyan, magenta, and yellow. (They do not use black which commercially is used for additional contrast.)

- Create your design with a computer or scan in a color picture. The right software can separate a color picture into dotted images for each of the process colors.

- Take your color picture to a commercial printer to have the separation work done.

OTHER USES FOR PROCESS COLORS

Do not be discouraged by this process! The Gocco Process Inks are vibrant colors for other uses. They can be used straight from the tube to ink a Master or mixed to make other colors. Expand your possibilities and mix Process Colors with any of the other colors. You will be pleased with the colors you can make by experimenting.

GREEN:
Mix bright, clear greens from lime to Kelly to emerald using varying proportions of Process Yellow and Process Cyan

ORANGE:
It takes only a small dab of Process Magenta to turn Process Yellow to orange.

PURPLE:
Process Magenta and Cyan in different proportions will make "berry stain" colors from raspberry to blueberry.

CLOTH INKS

Because these are water-based inks, they will not mix with the High Mesh Inks which are oil-water emulsion base. Pastel Cloth Inks are not available, but it is easy to mix them by adding a color to white.

It is easy to mix all colors, except a bright purple. The red and blue will make a grayed purple. Added to white, it will produce mauve.

COLORS CHANGE IN PRINTING

Gocco inks remain true to color when they dry, getting neither darker of lighter. However, they are not completely opaque. The color paper on which you print will affect ink color: Blue ink on yellow paper will look blue-green; white ink on red paper will be pink. Colors will be unchanged on white paper, and changed the most on bright or dark colors. Being aware of this, you can use it to your advantage rather than having an unexpected result.

EFFECTS TO TRY

- Print pastels on black paper. Do your original with black crayon on rough paper. Ink the exposed Master with pastel colors. The resulting Gocco print will look like colored chalk on a blackboard. Print a child's drawing this way.

- Try printing the same color ink as paper, e.g., red ink on red paper. This won't work for something meant to be legible, but it is effective for an all over design or background.

- Print with a color slightly different from the paper, e.g., Fluorescent Orange ink on red paper, or Fluorescent Green on Kelly green paper.

- The finish of Pearl and Metallic inks varies with the paper used. They look shinier on smooth, rather than on soft absorbent, paper. It was a surprise to see how pretty they looked on brown kraft lunch bags.

COLOR CHARTS

Spend time on a rainy day making your own color charts.

- Pencil rule 2" squares on plain white card stock weight paper.

- Mix small dabs of color on a paper palette.
- With a palette knife spread one color in each square.
- Note the proportions of each color swatch.
- Set charts aside to dry for a couple days.
- Put charts in your Gocco note book for handy reference.

Hint: Make a gold chart: mix 2 parts Gold with one part of each of the other colors. You will be surprised how nice some of the most unlikely combinations are, e.g. Gold and Fluorescent Pink, Gold and Brown, or Gold and Blue.

Sample color chart

INK BLOCK

There are two ways to apply more than one color to the Master: using Ink Block and butting colors together.

WHAT IS INK BLOCK?

Ink Block is a sheet of thin foam with a pressure sensitive adhesive on one side. Ink Block comes with the Printers, and is available separately in sheets $6^5/8''$ x $9^3/4''$. It is the easiest way to keep different colors of ink separated in multicolor printing. It fences ink in to keep it from spreading. Use Ink Block for designs that have separate areas of color.

HOW TO USE IT

- Plan Ahead! To use Ink Block, leave at least $1/4''$ between spots of different colors.

- Apply Ink Block to the Master after exposing the Master, but *before* inking.

- Lift up the Mylar top sheet of the Master. Cut a $1/8''$ wide strip of Ink Block. Peel off the backing paper and carefully place the sticky side of Ink Block onto inside of Master…the ink side.

- Do not put Ink Block right next to the design. Ink Block spreads out a bit in printing.

Ink Block separating flower design from HELLO

ADJOINING COLORS

Colors are placed touching each other when either there is no break in the design to allow room for a strip of Ink Block, or the space is too small. (Any part of the design covered by Ink Block will not print.)

It is surprising how effectively and precisely colors can be placed together. Since Gocco inks are thick, they do not readily blend the way watercolors do.

HOW TO BUTT COLORS TOGETHER

WHEN THERE IS A SMALL SPACE BETWEEN TWO PARTS OF THE DESIGN

It is important to remember that two colors of ink must be touching each other, equidistant between the two areas they are covering. The inks pushing against each other tend to maintain the line where they meet. If you leave space between the colors, one color may move farther than the other color, pushing it back over the place where you want the colors to meet.

WHEN A DESIGN IS CONTINUOUS

Careful attention to the placement of ink is most important. Colors must meet at *exactly* the place on the design where you intend the color to change. Suppose you are inking a daisy and want the center yellow and the petals white

- Ink the yellow center in an *even* circle.

- Place the white, making an even white doughnut, adjacent to the yellow center.

- If you place either color haphazardly, you will print a daisy with a blotchy, irregular center.

Daisy   "Donut" ink placement   Haphazard inking

LIMITATIONS OF ADJOINING COLORS

Joining colors together can give some impressive results, but, alas, the colors will not stay exactly where you put them. After about 30 printings the colors will drift. This is not always objectionable. A colorful bouquet of flowers looks fine if the colors move a bit, but not a face when a blue eye spreads to the nose or ear!

You are limited, no matter how careful you are, by how precisely you can ink a Master. For exact color placement you need to print the colors in multiple printings using two or more Masters. (See REGISTRATION, p. 136 for details.)

REINKING A MULTICOLOR MASTER

When you reink the Master, lifting up the Mylar top sheet will drag the ink out of place.

IF YOU USED INK BLOCK

Sometime the Mylar will drag the ink over the Ink Block. This is most apt to happen when there is still much ink on the Master, or if two Ink Blocked areas are close together. Carefully clean up misplaced ink.

IF YOU HAVE ADJOINING COLORS

Lifting up the Mylar sheet will disrupt carefully placed ink. Some designs are unaffected by colors that have moved a bit; blended colors may even enhance the design. Other designs need more precise placement of colors. For these you may have to clean the Master and reink it.

When reinking, it helps to place your original design under the Master as an inking guide, since it is harder to see a design once it has been inked.

- Tape original design to the work table.

- Place cleaned Master over design, aligning Master with design. You can see enough design on the Master to do this.

- Tape the Master down to the table to prevent frustration with jiggles as you are inking it.

POSSIBILITIES

Applying colors to the Master in different ways produces different effects. One design can take on several looks by varying the inking. They are all sure to impress the folks back home!

STRIPES

Ink in narrow or wide parallel stripes. Try placing stripes diagonally across a design.

CONFETTI

This is an adaptation from the pointillist school of painting. Ink the Master with small, closely spaced dots of different colors, about the size of miniature chocolate chips. Make the dots equal in size and evenly spaced. "HAPPY BIRTHDAY," "HAPPY NEW YEAR," and "CONGRATULATIONS" are enhanced with this technique. Your color scheme can range from exuberant to subtle, fluorescent to pastel, be analogous or complementary. Check your color wheel for ideas. Dots of Metallic Gold, Silver, and Bronze ink printed on dark blue paper make a festive look!

SWIRL

Start with a Master inked in a confetti pattern. Use a narrow spatula to gently stir through the dots of ink on the Master, swirling the colors around.

A variation: ink the Master in stripes of different colors. Drag a narrow spatula across the ink stripes. Make even parallel line passes across all the stripes. This is similar to making marbled paper and more fun than the mud pies of our childhood!

BLEND

Imagine a sunset with the colors gradually changing from yellow to orange to red. The key to a smooth gradation is to make many small color changes rather than a few large jumps. Abrupt color changes will be most obvious if the design is solid and continuous, and less obvious if there are breaks in the design. A smooth blend takes time and patience, but your results will be impressive.

- Start with yellow straight from the tube applied to the Master in a straight even bead along one end of the design.
- Squeeze some yellow ink on a palette and mix in just a bit of red.

- Put this color in an Ink Cone and make a narrow bead of ink next to the yellow already on the Master. You could use a spatula, but it is more difficult to control the amount and placement of ink on the Master.

- Squeeze any remaining ink out of the Ink Cone back on to the palette and mix in a bit more red, put this blend back in the Ink Cone and continue.

- Gauge the rate of color change so you end up with red at the end of the design.

- It is easy to ink the Master too heavily. Mix small quantities, and avoid applying a thick bead of ink.

RAINBOW

This is a variation of a Blend, using more colors. You can go through the whole rainbow or just a segment. Use colors at full intensity or blend a pastel rainbow with much white and little color. Mute the colors using shades or complements for a subdued rainbow colors. (Aren't you glad you bought that color wheel?)

Use rainbows and blends to print all-over patterns for a background with a bold design printed over the background in a second printing. (See REGISTRATION, PRINTING ON A BACKGROUND, p. 128.)

Not sure about the sequence of colors in the rainbow? Remember Roy G. Biv: red, orange, yellow, green, blue, indigo, violet. Yellow is so light and bright that it stands out too much when it is in the middle of the rainbow. You might want to start or end with yellow. Try yellow, green, blue, indigo, violet, red, and orange.

THINK AHEAD

Think ahead when inking a design in a rainbow. You don't want to come to the end of the design before you've gone through the whole spectrum.

- Make an inking guide by drawing the width of each color band on a piece of paper the size of your design. Label each color band to avoid mistakes. Tape the guide to your work surface.

- Expose the Master. Remove the original design from the Master. Place the Master over the ink guide and tape the Master in place. You will be able to see your guide through the Master.

- Now ink the Master following your guide.

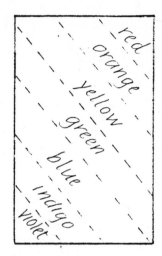

red

orange

yellow

green

blue

indigo

violet

Inking Guides

EMBOSSING

THE GENERAL IDEA

SPECIFICS

COLORS OF EMBOSSING POWDER

TROUBLESHOOTING

POSSIBILITIES

EMBOSSING

THE GENERAL IDEA

Thermographic embossing is one of the most exciting embellishments to add to your Gocco printing repertoire. This process involves sprinkling thermography powder over a freshly-printed Gocco image. Because ink of a Gocco-printed image is sticky when wet, thermography powder will easily adhere to the ink. Shake off excess powder. True to the *thermo* part of its name, thermography powder will quickly melt when heated to about 350°, changing from a sandy substance to a raised and shiny finish.

Transparent powder will make all colors raised and shiny. Some powders, such as gold and silver, are opaque. They will cover the ink and transform it to a shiny metallic finish.

Thermography powder is the traditional term, but it is now popularly called Embossing Powder. The distinction is only in words, so don't be confused. (Note that "dry embossing" is a different process. This uses a stencil-like template to impress a raised, three dimensional design into paper.)

SPECIFICS

PRINTING

Embossing Powder must be applied while the ink is wet. Gocco ink will stay wet long enough for you to print 10 to 15 cards at a time before you shake Embossing Powder over them. Note that printing on absorbent paper will dry faster than printing on glossy paper. Fine lines will dry quicker than large areas.

You do not have to melt the powder right away. You can shake powder on as many cards as you have room for and melt the powder later. Avoid stacking powdered cards. Unmelted powder can easily rub off when the ink dries.

PAPER

Many types of paper can be embossed, but generally, heavier text and cover stock papers are more suitable than

20 lb. copy-type paper that tends to buckle. However, even paper napkins can be embossed!

WAYS TO HANDLE EMBOSSING POWDER

The process will move along quickly if you can easily sprinkle powder on to the printed paper and then pour the remaining powder back in to a storage container when you are finished. Here are two suggestions, but you may have other ideas that suit your space and way of working:

A WIDE MOUTH CONTAINER

There are several shapes of suitable plastic containers. Consider a long narrow one: 3″ x 8″ x 3″. Hold a printed card over the container and use a spoon to "pour" powder over the card. Hold the card so that powder falls right back into the container. Using a container a bit wider than your paper makes this easy. Loosen excess powder by tapping card on the side of the container.

Apply embossing powder to paper

A SHAKER

An efficient method is to spread out about three or four feet of wax paper or newsprint. Print about fifteen cards placing them on the paper. Use a tablespoon or even a big salt shaker with extra large holes to quickly shake powder generously over all the cards.

Shake the excess powder off each card on to the wax paper. Snap the back of the card with your fingers to dislodge extra powder. When you've done all the cards, pick up the wax paper and pour the powder back into its container. It helps to have a container with a wide opening.

Repeat printing and powdering cards in lots of 15 or so. This method is a quick way to handle a large printing.

MELTING EMBOSSING POWDER

A good heat source for melting powder is as important as is an efficient method of sprinkling powder on the your cards. Once set up, you can easily process several hundred cards.

Whatever heat source you use, you want to heat the powder to about 350°. In a second or two, the powder will begin to bubble up. Just as it finishes bubbling, it melts and smoothes out. This is the moment when you take the card away from the heat. Finished, quick and easy! Allow a few seconds before stacking finished cards.

HEAT GUN

A heat gun is a popular convenient method of melting embossing powder. This is like a super hot hair dryer. It's a handy portable source of heat. Hold the nozzle of the gun about two or three inches from the powder. As powder in the immediate area melts and becomes shiny, move gun to the next spot.

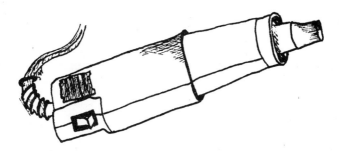

Heat Gun

- A home maintenance type of heat gun is available in hardware stores for stripping paint and thawing frozen pipes. You may already have one of these in your garage but you just never thought of using it for melting embossing powder! Look for a model that has variable heat control and a two-speed fan. (The fixed speed fan may blow your papers around.)

- A small craft model heat gun is available at rubber stamp stores. Small and light weight, a heat gun is handy to keep at your work space. They are perfect for small images, but are a bit slow on large Gocco images, especially B5 size prints.

OVEN BROILER

An oven broiler…yes, *broiled* paper is probably the quickest way to do large quantities. Set the rack (clean, so the paper doesn't get soiled) about 4" to 5" below the broiler coils. Keep rack pulled out a few inches so it is easy to grasp the rack to slide it in and out as your papers broil.

Broiler heat is uneven. Generally the center is hotter than the sides. Try placing three cards under the broiler: To the left, the right and then, last, the center. By the time all three cards are placed under the broiler, the left and right side cards will be finished *and* the center card will be just about done, too. Work fast, keep juggling three cards and very quickly you will have finished your project. This takes a little practice, but it will save you time on a big project.

You can alternate printing and powdering with broiling. Put the powdered cards near the broiler so you can get to them easily.

TOASTER OVEN

A small toaster oven will fit on a table near your printer. Set the oven on broil and place the paper about 3" below the heat unit. A small toaster oven may not be large enough to accommodate a big piece of paper or a B5-size image.

CONVENTIONAL OVEN

Embossed items can also be baked in a conventional oven. Set oven between 300° and 350°. Oven thermostats vary, so you'll need to experiment. Try 20 seconds. Oven heat is uneven, baking is slow, and requires frequent checking, so this is not an efficient method. Don't leave your paper in the oven when the phone rings!

MICROWAVE OVEN

The omni-present microwave comes to mind, but, alas, zapping in the microwave does *not* melt embossing powder!

OTHER HEAT SOURCES

These methods all provide bottom heat which does not melt the powder as well as top heat; the paper itself has to be heated before the powder will melt. Bottom heat is slow and suitable only for small jobs. Hold paper over the heat source until you see the powder melting.

- Coffee cup warmer
- Stove heating unit
- Hot plate, griddle
- Clothes iron
- Light bulb

COLORS OF EMBOSSING POWDER

The array of Embossing powders is dazzling: besides the popular transparent and metallics there is a wide selection of colors and powders with glitter added to them. Rubber stamp stores stock a variety of powders. This is a general overview of what is available.

Note: Using transparent powder over metallic ink will *lessen* the metallic look of the ink.

TRANSPARENT POWDERS

This includes plain transparent powder and transparent powders that have fine specks of colored glitter added. The transparent powders melt to a smooth glossy finish. The ink color under the powder will show.

METALLIC POWDERS

After transparent powders, metallic powders are the most popular. In addition to the gold, silver and copper powders, there are also colored metallics-quite a tempting array! Gocco Metallic Inks are attractive, but not quite as eye-catching as the raised, shiny finish of metallic embossing powders.

Metallic powders are generally opaque and will cover the color of the underlying ink. You can often use up odd colors of ink you've saved. (See MULTICOLOR PRINTING, USING STORED INK, p. 94.)

PEARLESCENT POWDERS

They add a pretty sheen to the ink. Some will mute and change the ink color, but not cover it completely. Others are opaque.

Pearlescent powders come in several colors. Lavender Pearl, for example, will change red to opalescent rose. These powders are often used commercially on wedding invitations.

COLORED POWDERS

You may wonder why one would even bother with colored powders, when colored inks with Transparent Embossing Powder give the same result. Yes, it does come out the same...on white paper, but not on black paper. The Gocco inks are not completely opaque. Colored ink on black paper will not look opaque. To make the color opaque on dark paper use colored embossing powder. This can produce some eye-popping results: Fluorescent orange pumpkins on black paper, hot pink hearts on purple paper!

WHITE POWDER

Gocco White Ink is not opaque. Use white embossing powder with White Ink to get an opaque white. Do not use transparent powder over white ink: it will make the white ink even *less* opaque.

White powder is so heavy and dense it looks as if it would cover all colors, but many colors will show through it. If you want white, be sure to use white ink with white powder. The Gocco Fluorescent Inks, especially, are prone to bleed through the white powder giving a pastel result. You may want to experiment with this effect.

TROUBLESHOOTING

WATCH THE HEAT!

- Too much heat and paper will absorb the embossing powder. The promised raised, shiny effect will disappear leaving a flat greasy look. Transparent powder is especially prone to this. Some papers such as brown lunch sacks are so absorbent they will soak up transparent powder even before the powder has finished melting.

- Metallic powders will not absorb into paper, but they will loose their shine if heated too long.
- Too much heat and the paper browns… we aren't in the paper toasting business! Be careful!
- Keep a pair of tongs handy to prevent burnt fingers.

SPECKS OF POWDER CLINGING TO PAPER

Embossing powder may cling stubbornly to rough or textured paper. Some linen finish paper holds powder like a magnet. Tiny specks of transparent powder may not show up, but specks of white powder on navy blue paper will be conspicuous. Before purchasing a large amount of new paper for a project, do a test first.

- Snapping your fingers on the back of the paper when you shake of excess powder will help.
- Powder will cling to oily finger prints: wash your hands before you begin.
- Powder will show up very tiny pin dots of ink that are otherwise barely visible. (See TROUBLESHOOTING, PIN DOTS, p. 221.)
- Powder may cling to shiny paper such as Cadillac Cover, a version of "static cling."

TEXTURE OF EMBOSSING POWDERS

Transparent powder melts to the smoothest and shiniest finish. If powder is still grainy or sandy feeling after heating it, the powder has not completely melted. It is not done, so "cook" it a little more.

The pigments in other colors prevent them from being as smooth as transparent powder. Heat powder until it has stopped bubbling and is smoothing out. At this point the powder is as smooth as it will be.

POSSIBILITIES

This, finally, is the fun part. Now you can play and experiment.

MIXED MEDIA

Once an image is embossed, it is easy to add additional color with water color, gouache, or felt markers. Melted powder is a perfect resist, so it will repel water colors.

Coloring inside the lines has never been so easy! This is a creative and easy way to add more color to a card. By changing colors, each card will be unique.

- Do an outlined letter with gold embossing; fill in the letter with water color or gouache.

- Print an outlined cluster of balloons in black with transparent embossing. Color in each balloon with different colors.

- Color in balloons with embossing pens. Embossing pens come in clear and colors. Embossing powder will adhere to embossing pen "ink" while ink is wet. These pens allow you to emboss in several colors on one card.

- Consider a water color wash over the whole card. The water will roll right off the embossed portion.

MIXING POWDERS

If just one kind of embossing is fun, think of how exciting it is to mix powders!

- Mix about one part silver and three parts transparent powder. Try this glittery mix on marine scenes or frost-covered trees.

- Add some metallic powder to a fluorescent or colored powder: copper and orange powder; silver and blue powder; gold and red powder.

- Add gold or silver to opaque white powder.

- Mix gold and silver powders to make a warmer gold or cooler silver, or mix gold and copper.

PARTIAL POWDERING

You don't need to cover the entire image with embossing powder.

- Pour copper powder over only one third of a large red-orange fall leaf.

- Print HAPPY BIRTHDAY and pour silver powder over one part and gold over the rest.

SPECIAL EFFECTS

It is easy to experiment with different paper and powders. This is a good justification for keeping a variety of papers and powders on hand. You will be amazed at how easily one design is transformed. An hour of printing can easily become an afternoon of happy "play."

- Some very lightweight papers work surprisingly well: Silk Span with gold embossing looks like a gold image almost suspended on the sheer paper. (Silk Span is an inexpensive paper available at art supply stores.)

- Embossing powders can be layered, e.g., emboss a starry background in silver; over this print MY STARS in navy blue and then emboss the second printing with transparent powder. The first embossing will not be harmed by a second exposure to heat

- Note: If you are doing a second printing over an unembossed background, be sure the ink of the first printing is thoroughly dry before sprinkling powder over the second printing. Embossing powder will readily stick to ink that feels nearly dry.

- Florists ribbon can be embossed. Use the ribbon for streamers, in a bouquet, a runner down a table. Experiment with the heat source. Some florist ribbon shrivels up under heat. Try using bottom heat instead. Hold the ribbon over an iron, pulling ribbon across the bottom of an upturned iron.

Using an iron to melt embossing powder

- Fabric can be embossed, but it will absorb much of the powder, so there will not be the same raised shiny effect as embossing on paper. Mostly, embossing helps to bond ink to the fabric making the fabric more washable. *Do not* put embossed fabric in the dryer, as the powder will melt and rub off on the dryer and other garments!

MIXED MEDIA

PAPER EMBELLISHMENTS

DIMENSIONAL EFFECTS

MIXED MEDIA

Gocco printing is wonderful, but it is the beginning, not the end, of your creative endeavors. There are many avenues you can explore in combining Gocco printing with other media.

PAPER EMBELLISHMENTS

Gocco printing can be combined with just about any other method of making marks on paper.

- Photo copy a news letter or flyer and add a colorful Gocco printed masthead, illustration, or color spot. Use this technique to add color to something too large to print completely in your printer. Are you sending a holiday newsletter? Print it on a photo copier and add a colorful Gocco-Printed salutation.

Gocco print a color spot on a newsletter.

- Commercially print a large poster and stamp a color accent with the Gocco Stamping Kit for cloth. (See STAMP KIT FOR CLOTH, PRINTING ON OTHER SURFACES, p. 171)

- Use metallic markers to add a border around a card. Outline a large Gocco-printed initial letter with a metallic marker, add gold highlights to autumn leaves, dots of silver to snowflakes.

- Glitter glue is another handy item. Use it to outline or fill in a selected Gocco-printed image. Add frost to

winter trees, red glitter to Valentine hearts, sparkle to
fireworks.

- Sheets or strips of foil bonded to a Mylar carrier
  sheet will adhere to writing made with a glue pen.
  This is an easy way to add a shiny metallic look.
  Allow glue to dry to a tacky finish, then place foil dull
  side to adhesive and burnish foil with a fingernail or
  the back of a spoon. Lift up Mylar and foil will have
  adhered to adhesive.

- Incorporate stickers with your design. Balloon
  stickers can float above HAPPY BIRTHDAY. "Tie" the
  stickers to the letters with pen-drawn "string."

Balloon stickers "tied" to Gocco design

- Colored pencils can add detail and variety to your
  work.

- Use water colors to make a light colored wash on
  watercolor paper, then Gocco print over this
  background. Try this for seascapes or sunsets.

- Rubber stamped images can be a great accent for a
  Gocco printed design. Keep your stamps in sight
  and you will find many ways to combine them with

Gocco printing. This category alone can keep you busy for hours, days.

Rubber stamps accent a Gocco print

- Combine watercolors or marking pens with thermographed images. (See EMBOSSSING CHAPTER p. 69).
- Use the new embossing pens to add color to Gocco prints, e.g. color in Gocco-printed outlines of balloons with embossing pens and add embossing powders. This adds not only color but texture to a design.
- Wonder Tape is another new product: a heat-resistant double stick tape that can add lines or borders to cards. The adhesive tape is a base to hold foil, embossing powder, or flocking powder.

DIMENSIONAL EFFECTS
This list is just to whet your desire to experiment!

- Emboss paper to give it a raised effect. Emboss a dove on a card printed with the word "Peace." (*Emboss* in this case refers to impressing a dimensional design into paper.)
- Fun Flock is a flocking powder sold at rubber stamp stores. Write with a glue pen, sprinkle on the flocking powder. Let dry a few hours, shake off powder and you'll have a flocked design. Use to add white snow to a Gocco-printed evergreen tree.
- Add a red pompom to a printed clown's hat, or nose, a lace ruffle around his neck, and sequins on his clothes. "Tie" a bow around a teddy bear's neck.

Rick rack, feathers, glue-on-eyes are other fun decorations to use.

Add a pom-pom or bow to a card

• Pop-up cards are fun. (See APPENDIX, BIBLIOGRAPHY, p. 235 for books on making pop-up cards.)

MAXIMIZING MATERIALS

PRINT MASTERS

INK

PAPER

MAXIMIZING MATERIALS

Gocco Printing, already a bargain compared to commercial printing, can be even more economical by recycling Masters and Ink.

PRINT MASTERS

EXPOSING A PRINT MASTER

FILLING UP THE ENTIRE MASTER

Get the most out of your Masters before you expose them. When exposing a Master, avoid putting one small design in the middle of a Master. Fill up Master with other designs so you are using the entire image area. Keep a file folder of filler designs: clip art, etc., that you collect and save for just this purpose. Keep in mind the maximum image area for a Master. (See PREPARING DESIGNS, p. 29)

- B6: 4" x 5³/₄"
- B5: 6"x 9"

LAYING OUT YOUR DESIGNS

Layout sheets are a handy way to control the various designs you are using to fill up a Master. Cut sheets of plain white paper or non-photo blue grid paper the size of the image area. (Cut several sheets and keep them with your printer, so they will always be at hand.) Use Tack-A-Note glue stick or regular glue stick to hold the design pieces in place.

Using lay out sheets

INK BLOCK

You don't need to print all images on the Master at the same time. Remember Ink Block? Ink Block will contain ink so it doesn't spread. Put Ink Block on the Master after exposing, but before inking.

Ink Block confines ink to just one part of Master

Forget? Ink has spread, and now parts of another design are printing? Here's an easy fix: Place a Post-A-Note or two on the outside of Master covering the unwanted area that is printing. The Post-A-Note will not harm the Master, but remember to remove it when you store the Master.

SAVING AN INKED PRINT MASTER

If you are on a roll, printing furiously, but are interrupted by "life," you can save your inked Master. Wrap Master in aluminum foil. Don't use plastic wrap. Plastic wrap can ruin a Master by adhering to the shiny saran coating on the outside of the Master and pulling it off when you unwrap the Master, ruining your design.

Stored in a cool place, a Master will keep for several days...but not forever. (We all know how time has a way of getting away from us.)

When you are ready to resume printing, unwrap Master and print a few copies on scrap paper. You may find that the Master needs reinking.

INKED MASTER WON'T PRINT

Oh, oh, did you store a Master for so long that ink has dried in the Master? You can still save the Master with Master Cleaner or Goop (an automotive hand cleaner) (See APPENDIX, SUPPLIES, p. 240)

- Spread a thin layer of Master Cleaner outside the Master. After about fifteen minutes, wipe off Cleaner with paper toweling and try printing a few copies on scrap paper. If ink has dried only slightly, this may soften it and allow you to continue printing.

- If the ink has dried thoroughly, put a generous layer of Master Cleaner on outside of Master; lift up Mylar top sheet and spread another layer over the dried ink. Wrap Master again and let Cleaner "stew" for a couple of hours and then clean Master. You may need to repeat this process to completely clean a Master.

- Paint thinner or mineral spirits will also work, but they smell and are not as mild as Master Cleaner.

CLEANING PRINT MASTERS

When you are finished printing, you can clean the Master and save it indefinitely. Even if you won't be using this design again, there may be other images on the Master that you'll want to print later.

- Place Master Mylar side up, with a piece of scrap paper under it. Lift up Mylar. Scrape ink off the Master and Mylar top sheet with a plastic spatula, a piece of card stock or an old credit card. Avoid anything sharp.

Scrape ink off Master with an old credit card

- Wipe remaining ink from Master and Mylar with paper toweling.

- Apply a light coating of Master Cleaner to inside surface of the Master. Let sit for a few minutes, place another clean piece of scrap paper under Master and wipe Cleaner off with toweling. Discard paper under Master and replace it with a clean piece, and wipe once more. It is not necessary to remove all traces of ink. Scrubbing can wear out the Master, but it is important to remove enough ink so a residue of ink does not clog the tiny holes in the Master. Check by holding the Master up to light. You should be able to see light through the image area when the Master is clean.

- Mineral spirits may be used instead of Master Cleaner. Do not use lacquer thinner or acetone. They will dissolve the Master.

- See STAMP KIT FOR CLOTH, CLEAN UP, p. 168 for cleaning Stamp Ink for Cloth from the Master.

STORING CLEANED PRINT MASTERS

Set up a system for filing Print Masters so they are ready to reuse. Here are some ideas.

FILING MASTERS

Paper "file folders" are an easy way protect and organize a growing collection of Masters.

- For the B6 Printer, fold an $8^1/_2$" x 11" sheet of paper in half crosswise.

Paper "file folder" over Master

- For the B5 Printer, fold a sheet of 11" x 17" paper in half crosswise, tape two pieces of $8^1/_2$" x 11" paper together along the 11" side and fold along taped seam.

- Print your design on the folded paper, fold at the top. Do this when you *begin* your printing so you won't forget. Make a note on the paper if there are other images on the Master besides the printed one.
- When you are finished, put cleaned Print Master inside its paper folder.
- Use a box to file your Masters. The printed image allows quick identification, and with the folded edge up, it is easy to flick through your file.
- When you have accumulated a couple dozen Masters, add Post-A-Note divider tabs and sort your Masters by categories.
- You could also color code your Masters by using different color paper folders.

OTHER METHODS
Envelopes securely hold your reference notes, a printed sample, and a copy of the original design.

- For B6 Masters, use 6" x 9" envelopes
- For the B5 Masters, use 10" x 13" envelopes.
- Color code envelopes with a marking pen stripe along the top edge.
- Ziploc bags work, but be careful to place a piece of paper between bag and Master. Print your design on this paper for easy identification.
- Lunch bags work for B6 Masters; larger sacks, for B5 Masters.

REUSING YOUR SAVED MASTERS
Now that you have saved your Masters, let's consider creative ways to reuse them.

- Reink Master in a different color, or print on a different color paper.
- Print a child's name on different items, e.g. stationery, envelopes, lunch sacks, a tag for a package.
- Use embossing powder on the image.

- Change the position of a design: top, bottom, diagonally?
- Combine an old design with a new one, e.g., print your old design on a new textured background. (See REGISTRATION, PRINTING ON A BACKGROUND, p. 128)
- Print only part of an image. On Master with a whole heart; print only 1/2 of the heart… "Don't be half hearted." Put a Post-A-Note on the outside of the Master to cover half the heart image.

Post-A-Note covering half of heart on outside of Master

INK

AMOUNT OF INK

When you start printing, you will notice that the ink spreads out on the Master beyond the design. Next time, before inking Master, circle the design with Ink Block. A fence of Ink Block around the design will confine the ink, preventing it from spreading. You will get more prints before needing to reink.

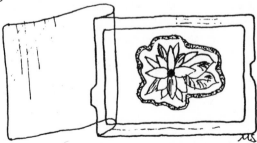

Ink Block surrounds the design

SHORT CUTS

If you run out of ink at a corner or an edge of the Master, you can lift up part of the Mylar top sheet without disturbing the rest of the ink.

Often a Master runs out of ink at the end of the Master where the Mylar attaches to the cardboard frame. (Ink always seems to run out in the hardest places to reach!) Pull the Mylar from the cardboard frame and add more ink.

Need just a few more copies? Pumping the Printer up and down a few time my yield several more prints. You may not have to add more ink. Hold the Master up to the light after lifting up the Mylar sheet. Light will shine through the areas where ink is thin. Redistribute remaining ink to cover bare spots. Use a small spatula to move ink that has spread beyond the design area.

PRINTING A SERIES

Suppose you are printing personalized stationery for several friends, using the same ink color. Here are some ideas to save time:

- Two or three names and addresses will fit on one B6 Master, more on a B5 Master.

Print three projects from just one Master

- Ink the first name, print, clean Master. Save the ink you scrape off the Master.
- Reapply this ink to the next name on the Master.

- Continue, adding more ink as needed, until you are finished. You will have used much less ink than if you added all new ink for each name.

STORING INK

Many people don't realize that they can save ink cleaned from a Master. Stored ink will keep for a few weeks in a cool place. Ink stored in a warm place will mold...phew!

- Wrap ink in an aluminum foil packet: Use a small square of foil. Place mound of ink in middle of foil, wrap foil tightly around ink, squeezing out air. Place a dab of ink on outside of packet to indicate color. The advantage to this method is that it is easy to reuse the ink; unfold packet, smooth out foil, and scrape off ink. The foil also makes a handy mini-palette.

Open up foil packet and use as mini-palette

- Plastic wrap is transparent, but ink dries out faster in plastic wrap than in foil.

- Store ink in small containers: e.g., 35 mm film containers, pill holders, fast food sauce containers. It sometimes can be awkward scooping ink out of these small containers. Use a narrow strip of mat board for a scoop.

USING STORED INK

Now that you've gone to the trouble of saving your ink, don't ignore it!

- Saved ink is a great excuse to experiment with mixing colors. Even if you don't want to save ink, experiment mixing colors scraped off a Master before discarding the ink. Mix small amounts of ink on a sheet of white paper, and you'll learn a lot about colors!

- Odd colors are good to use these when you are working with gold, copper, or silver embossing powders. These powders are quite opaque and will cover the ink color.

PAPER

CONSERVING YOUR GOOD PAPER

Once a Master is inked and you are ready to print, see REGISTRATION for techniques on positioning your paper, so you can get your image where you want it. Then you won't waste your good paper getting set up.

RECYCLING

- Scrap paper or junk mail comes in handy. Place scrap paper under the Master when you are cleaning it.
- Make your first test prints on scrap paper.

PHOTO SCREEN

DOT SCREENS

PHOTOGRAPHS

POSSIBILITIES

PHOTO SCREEN

The Photo Screen is a versatile accessory. It not only helps in printing photos, but has other graphic uses.

DOT SCREENS

- The Gocco Photo Screen comes in a packet containing two dot screens that are 65 line and measure $3\frac{1}{2}''$ x $5\frac{1}{2}''$. These screens are clear Mylar covered with tiny white dots...65 lines of dots per inch.
- There are dot screens of other densities besides the Gocco Photo Screen. Graphic departments in art stores carry dot screens. They are also called copy screens. They come in 65 line and 85 lines of dots per inch. Experiment with various copy screens for different effects.

PHOTOGRAPHS

Do not use photographs to expose a Master, because even black photographs do not contain carbon. To use a photograph, photocopy it first.

SELECTING A PHOTOGRAPH

- Choose a photo with good contrast of light and dark tones, either black and white or color.
- Select a photo without a lot of small details, e.g., a close-up of one person works better than a distant group shot of several people.

PREPARING THE PHOTOGRAPH

PHOTO COPYING

Copy machines vary in the detail they reproduce from photos. Try several copiers to see the differences. Experiment with the light/dark setting, too.

There are two ways to photocopy a photograph, with or without the Dot Screen.

- Using a Dot Screen, the copy of the photo will be less harsh and appear to have gray shades due to the dot pattern. A screened copy of a person is more flattering than an unscreened one. It is similar to the half tones produced by professional printers.

- Place Dot Screen on glass of copy machine.

- Next center photograph face down on top of Dot Screen. Photo copy to produce a dotted copy of the photo, similar to a newspaper photo.

- Lighter photo copies produce the best results, since each tiny dot in the photo copy will print a bit darker in the Gocco.

- Photographs copied without a screen will have strong black and white contrasts but little shading. They tend to look stark. Setting the copier set on light so the gray areas do not reproduce will accentuate this. Buildings or trees get an interesting skeletal look copied without a screen. This technique does not flatter people!

Photo without screen

Photo with screen

Screen background cropped from photo

CROPPING

After making the photo copy, trim away the distracting background, especially around a person's head.

PRINTING

- Remember to use the Blue Filter with photo copies.

- Choose ink color for printing a picture of a person carefully. Green may not be the best choice! Rather than black, mix a charcoal gray or tan. The new translucent Water Color Effect Ink in Camel Tan will produce a light sepia effect that is hauntingly subtle. Also striking is a taupe blend of Camel Tan and Moon Gray.

- Print a face in all one color rather than trying to ink the eyes and mouth in different colors.

- When printing, experiment with the amount of pressure you use. The print may be better if you use a little less pressure than usual.

POSSIBILITIES

PHOTOGRAPHS

- Print stationery with a child's photo. Maybe this will encourage letter writing.

- Personalize lunch sacks with a photo rather than a name.

- Print Christmas cards, baby announcements, or birthday cards using children's photographs.

- Make party decorations, place cards, name tags, with the honored guest's picture.

OTHER USES

- Screen large solid areas makes them less dense. Exposing and printing large solid areas can be difficult with the Gocco but the screen changes a solid area into a dotted one. Printed, a screened area will look almost solid. Photo copy a design placing the dot screen between the design and photo copier just as you did with a photograph.
(See TROUBLESHOOTING, EXPOSING LARGE SOLID AREAS, p. 222.)

Screen large solid areas

- The Dot Screen can lighten textures and designs. Use for background printing with a bolder design printed over the background.

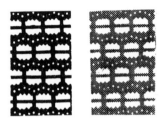

Screen a background

- Lighten lines with a Dot Screen. Suppose you are printing lines on recipe cards. Screen the lines so they will print more subtly, as dotted lines rather than solid lines.

Lighten lines by screening

FELT PRINTING

SUPPLIES

HOW IT WORKS

NOTES

POSSIBILITIES

FELT PRINTING

Felt will add an appealing tactile quality to your printing, making the image raised and fuzzy. Do you remember Fuzzy Wuzzy children's books? The Print Gocco Felt Sheet box contains everything you need.

SUPPLIES

- Eight sheets of felted paper 4" x 6", two each pink, aqua, yellow, and white
- Container of adhesive powder
- Instructions

HOW IT WORKS

This is a four step process of printing, sprinkling on powder, melting powder, and ironing on the felt paper.

- Print as usual.

- Sprinkle adhesive powder over wet ink and shake off excess.

- Melt powder using embossing procedures. (See EMBOSSING, p. 69) The adhesive powder will melt flat and only partly shiny unlike embossing powder, which melts to a raised, glossy finish.

- Place a felt sheet, fuzzy side down, over the image. Iron over felt sheet with a medium hot iron for about twenty seconds. To prevent the felt sheet from shifting, press, lift, and replace iron rather than sliding it. Felt adheres to the paper with a combination of heat and pressure. Allow paper to cool before pulling off felt sheet. Voila...fuzzies!

NOTES

- Ink color will show through the felt, e.g., a brown bear will become tan with application of white felt over brown ink. A yellow chicken will be brighter with yellow felt over yellow ink.

- For an even application of felt, do not reuse portions of a used sheet.

- Embossing powder will not work as a substitute for the adhesive powder. There is plenty of adhesive powder for all felt sheets in the kit.

- Felt papers sold in art stores do not work. This felt adheres to the printed paper so securely that it can not be pulled off the paper after ironing without tearing.

- Use felt finish florist ribbon as a substitute for felt sheets. Do not confuse this ribbon with velvet ribbon!

POSSIBILITIES

The first thing that may come to mind for felt printing is fuzzy chickens and bunnies, but don't stop there.

- Try white snow flakes, clouds, or fuzzy sheep.

- Consider emphasizing the contrast in textures between the matte-finish felt and very shiny paper such as Krome Kote. A white snow-covered tree in white felt on shiny white paper is striking.

White felt images on shiny white paper

- Print personalized stationery with three bold initials in felt. Use this as a cover for a small book.
- Print felt on fabric or ribbons. Use this for items that will not be laundered.
- Print *HEART FELT WISHES* in pink ink with pink felt over it.

Heart Felt Wishes

REGISTRATION

GRID GUIDES

PAPER PLACEMENT

REPEAT PRINTS OF A SINGLE IMAGE

LARGER DESIGNS

PRINTING ON A BACKGROUND

PLAID

MASKING REGISTRATION

EXACT REGISTRATION

ALMOST REGISTRATION

PROCESS COLOR PRINTING

POSSIBILITIES

REGISTRATION

Registration, in the printing world, is printing an image in correct alignment. Print two or more images on top of, or adjacent to, each other to make a unified design. In this section we will consider several variations of multiple printings and easy alignment techniques.

GRID GUIDES

The first step in registration and multiple printing is controlling the placement of paper for single printing.

FOAM BASE

A piece of grid paper attached to the Printer's Foam Base can be helpful in registration as well as in single image printing.

- Cut several pieces of graph paper the size of the Foam Base. You'll need only one piece for now; save the others so they'll be handy for next time. Grid paper size:
  B6: 4$\frac{1}{4}$" x 6$\frac{1}{8}$"
  B5: 7" x 9"

- Even though the Foam Base is tacky, it is not sticky enough to hold paper securely. For registration you don't want your printing guide to move! Place two or three strips of double stick tape across the Foam Base. Attach grid paper to Base.

Grid paper guide on Foam Base of B-6 Printer

- When you are finished, remove the grid paper and tape, and get ready for your next project.
- Put inked Master in Printer and print image on the grid paper attached to base. Allow a few minutes for ink to dry so it doesn't smudge on to the back of your printing paper. If you just can't wait, spread a piece of Kleenex over the grid paper.

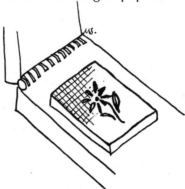

Print image on grid paper

- To hold your good paper in place, rub some Tack-A-Note, repositionable glue stick, on the grid paper. A little Tack-A-Note will keep paper from moving and will not smudge your paper.
- An advantage of having the image printed on the base is that you can move your good paper around on the base to get an idea of where the image will print. Move your paper too far; it will not cover the image on the base. You will see immediately that you will get only a partial image on your paper, unless you want only a partial image. If your paper is a bit transparent, you can see through it and know exactly where the image will print.
- Draw pencil guide lines on the grid to mark where to place the paper.

PAPER PLACEMENT

Attaching grid paper to the Foam Base and printing on the grid is handy, but it is just a beginning. You may not be sure where you want to print an image. It is fun to experiment. The look will change when you vary placement of paper.

TRACING PAPER ALIGNMENT

Often good paper is too opaque to see through it to the image printed on the grid base. Use tracing paper in place of good printing paper. (You don't want to waste your good paper experimenting.)

- Cut several pieces of tracing paper the same size as your printing paper.

- Place the tracing paper over the image printed on the grid paper attached to base. Move the tracing paper around to explore new positions.

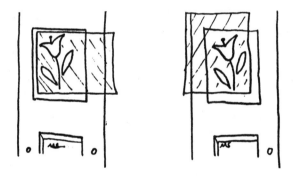

Different placements of tracing paper in Printer

- You can print on the tracing paper just to be sure. Doesn't look right? Try another, you are not wasting your printing paper.

- Make pencil guide marks on grid paper/base around corners of the tracing paper to indicate where to place your printing paper.

Pencil guide marks at corners

- When you are satisfied, print away!

PRINTING ON PAPER
LARGER THAN THE FOAM BASE

Sometime the paper you are printing on is larger than the Foam Base, and covers the base so you can't make any guide marks on the base. You need a larger base! Here's how to make a larger surface for the Foam Base:

- Glue an 8½" x 11" sheet of grid paper to a sheet of card stock, or similar weight paper to stiffen the grid paper. If you are printing on a very large piece of paper, you may need an even larger base. Do not use a rigid paper such as mat board for a base. It will eliminate the springy effect of the Foam Base pushing up against the paper when printing.

- Securely attach grid guide to Foam Base with double stick tape.

- Print your image on the new base as before. The base should be large enough for guide lines.

- Position your printing paper on your new larger grid base. Make guide lines on grid base for placement of printing paper.

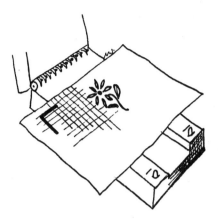

Larger grid guide attached to Foam Base

- PLAN AHEAD: Make sure the large paper you are want to use will fit in Printer. Watch out for the two posts at the front of the B6 Printer. They punch messy holes in paper.

MYLAR OVERLAY ALIGNMENT

- Use the grid base you used for printing on larger paper in the preceding section.
- Cut a piece of clear Mylar the same size as the grid base, placing Mylar on top of grid base. (Mylar, acetate, or a photo copier transparency will all work.)

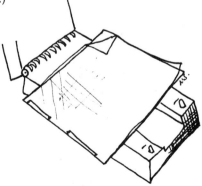

Mylar attached to grid base

- Securely tape Mylar to grid base along the left side of the base. The Mylar sheet will open to the left, just like the cover of a book.
- Attach grid base securely to Foam Base of Printer with double stick tape.
- Fold Mylar back over grid to "close" the book.
- Print right on Mylar sheet.

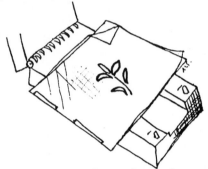

Image printed on Mylar overlay

- Slide printing paper under the Mylar sheet, moving paper around to where you want the image to print.
- Hold paper in place as you fold Mylar sheet back to the left. Mark position of this paper on the grid base. This is where you will place each piece of paper for printing. The Mylar stay folded out of the way to the left.

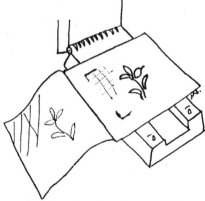

Placement marks on grid base

- Reuse Mylar by wiping the image off with Goop.
  (See APPENDIX, NON GOCCO SUPPLIES)

PRECISE PAPER PLACEMENT

A template you can fit paper against is more accurate and quicker than lining paper up along pencil lines. These techniques will be important when you get to more exact methods of registration. Here are two easy methods:

POSITIONING "L"

- Cut an "L" shape that is about 2" wide in both it's horizontal and vertical parts and about 6" tall. Use index or cover stock weight paper.

- Attach "L" to the grid base with glue stick or double stick tape. Place "L" so that the printing paper fits into inside corner of the "L".

- Print a couple trials on scrap paper. Make final adjustments before glue sets. You're on your way!

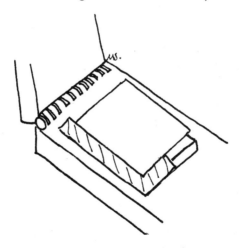

Positioning "L" attached to Foam Base

SCREEN PRINTING TABS

Screen printers use this method. Like the "L" this method assures accurate placement of each sheet of paper.

- Determine where you want to place your paper for printing. Secure paper with a dab of glue stick in the center, not at the edges.

- Cut four 4" long strips of 1" wide masking tape for tabs. Place two tabs along one side of the paper and two along the bottom. Your printing paper will fit into the tabs the way it fits into the "L".

- Place first tab along left side about 2" up from the lower left corner.

- Hold tape on the base, horizontally, sticky side down. Place 1" of tape under the printing paper. Three inches of tape will extend freely to the left. Keep this 3" part from sticking to the base.

- Fold the 3" part of the tape, sticky side up, to the right. Sharply crease tape along edge of the paper.

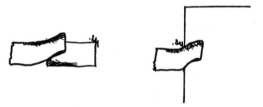

Screen printing tabs

- One inch to the right of this crease, fold the tape back to the left over itself, sticky sides together. You are making a 1" tape tab that folds to the right over the printing paper. Crease tape so it forms sharp creases and a flat tab.

- The last 1" of tape will continue to the left on to the grid paper base anchoring down the tab.

- Make another tab a few inches above the first one, depending upon paper size.

- Make two more tabs along bottom of paper. The first tab will be about 2" to the right of the lower left corner; and the second, a few more inches to the right.

Screen printing tabs attached to Foam Base

- You can now place your paper under the tabs so each sheet will be in exactly the same place for printing.
- Take care when making tabs so they will not cover any area where the image will print on the paper. You can trim a tab if part of it is in the way.

REPEAT PRINTS OF A SINGLE IMAGE

A single image has more possibilities than you might think. Start with one image of a flower. Now imagine several flowers printed in an overlapping pattern. A single flower is transformed into more than the sum of its parts!

ALONG A STRAIGHT LINE

Repeat one image at even intervals across a page. Images can be separate or overlap slightly for a feeling of depth. Use a narrow, long strip of paper for a flower border.

This paper is probably too long to fit under the Mylar sheet used in the Mylar overlay alignment on page. Use the TRACING PAPER ALIGNMENT described on p. 115, or just estimate...after all, flowers don't measure where they grow.

PRINTING FIRST FLOWER

- Prepare a Master with a single flower. Print one flower on the grid paper on Foam Base of Printer.

- Cut a few pieces of tracing paper the same size as your printing paper.

- Print a flower at the left end of the tracing paper, just as you will do on your printing paper. Align your paper along the left and bottom sides of Foam Base of Printer.

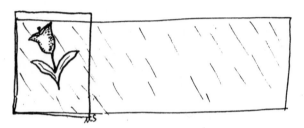

Printing first flower

- Print the first flower on all the papers, placing each paper in the same place.

PRINTING SECOND FLOWER

- Place the tracing paper with a flower on it over the flower printed on the grid base, but move the paper to the *left*. This is when you decide how far apart the first and second flowers will be: will they overlap a little, just touch, or have a space between them?

Printing second flower

- You can continue printing yards of flower border ... it does get addictive!

- Yards? Yes, yards. Print on ribbon or wide adding machine tape. Make baby shower garlands, table streamers, hair ribbons.

HINTS

- When setting papers aside to dry, keep them in the order printed. When you print the second flower, start with the first papers printed, since they will have had longer to dry. The ink from the first printing must be dry before doing the second print. Otherwise, the wet ink from the first printing will transfer to the Master and in turn transfer to your paper.

- Print flowers one, three and five in the first printing, let them dry, then print flowers two and four in the second printing. This means to print five flowers you handle the paper only two times rather than five times, and you don't have to wait for each flower to dry before printing overlapping flowers.

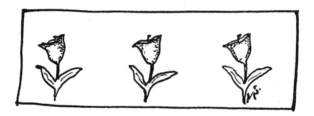

Printing alternate flowers

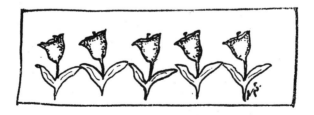

Second printing to fill in flowers

ALONG A STAGGERED LINE

These are variations of the straight line technique in which the base line changes.

- Mark two base lines, one line above the other. Flowers one, three and five are printed with the paper placed on the upper base line. Print flowers two and four with the paper placed along the lower base line. What was a straight line of flowers changes into a border with some flowers behind the others.

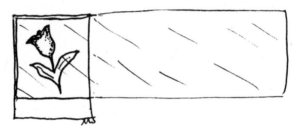

Guide for printing flowers on a staggered line

Flowers printed alone staggered line

- The base line might be a wavy line changing the border of straight flowers into a garland. You probably don't need to measure for this; just eye ball it.
- Print birds in flight, printing a bird along a "moving" line.

COLOR VARIATIONS

The examples above have assumed printing the same image in the same colors. Now imagine printing the same image, but changing colors between printings. Print a long narrow card: "Happy, Happy, Happy, Happy, Happy Birthday." This can be a hanging card or folded up in a zigzag accordion style.

- Make a Master with "Happy Birthday". Put Ink Block on Master between Happy and Birthday.
- Ink just Happy in yellow ink printing one yellow Happy at the top of each card.
- Use a spatula to remove the remaining yellow from the Master. Add green, making a yellow green. Reink Master. Print a couple copies on scrap paper to work the last of the yellow ink from the Master.
- Print the second Happy in yellow green under the yellow Happy.
- Remove this ink from Master adding more green, and repeat process. Continue printing Happy changing color each time working from yellow, to green to blue, to purple, possibly ending with Birthday being in an intense purple. (See MAXIMIZING MATERIALS, STORING INK, p. 94.)

Happy birthday on Master and printed result

SHADOW IMAGE

Print an image in pale colors, then partially overlap the pale image with the same image in a brighter color creating a pale shadow along one side of the bright color.

- Print pale shadow first. Mark paper position on grid lines.

Print of shadow with paper position marks for both printings

- Clean the Master and reink with a bolder color. Reposition paper for second printing. This is where grid paper on the Foam Base helps. Move printing paper to the left one square on the grid ($^1/_8$"), but keep paper on the same base line. This gives a subtle shadow offset to the left just enough to give a suggestion of depth.

Second printing of brighter color with paper on second position mark

LARGER DESIGNS

Print larger designs than will fit on one Print Master by breaking design into smaller parts. You may have to modify the design so it can be divided without looking cut apart. It is difficult, for example, to make a line look continuous when you print it in segments. However it is easy to print a newsletter in several printings by breaking it into paragraphs. Do a very long narrow piece such as a calendar printing each month separately.

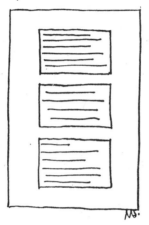

Larger design printed in three sections

PRINTING ON A BACKGROUND

This is an easy way to add texture to a project. Generally the background should not compete with the foreground. Print a background of muted color and pattern and over it a bold foreground in a contrasting color.

BACKGROUND SUGGESTIONS

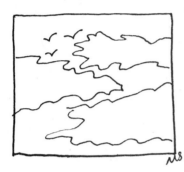 

Print a bright rainbow over light clouds

Print silhouettes of palm trees over a sunset

- Save your background Masters. Use them again in different colors.
- Backgrounds can be thermographed with embossing powder and then printed over, or just the second printing can be embossed. If you are embossing the second printing, be sure the

background print is thoroughly dry so no embossing powder adheres to it. (See EMBOSSING CHAPTER, p. 69.)

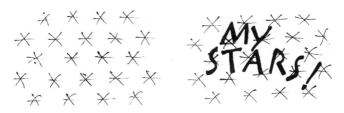

Star background with MY STARS printed over background

- A quarter inch grid makes a good background. Print bold writing diagonally across grid, or other similar texture.

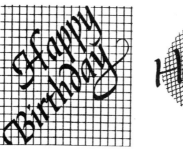 

Ideas for grid background printing

MAKING TEXTURED BACKGROUNDS

There are many sources of textures for background printing.

- Make rubbings from leaves, coins, window screening, or sand paper. Place paper over object and rub with a carbon pencil or black crayon. Shake off pencil dust before making the Master. If you didn't use carbon black, photo copy the rubbing.

- Wrapping paper, marbled paper, striped or tweed fabric, all can be photo copied then Gocco Printed. Note: Avoid using copyrighted designs.

- Photo copy black lace, or use white lace placed over black paper for a reverse image of the lace.

Photo copied lace and fabric

- Have you thought of copying hair? Cut hair from the local hair salon, or place your own long hair in a copier! It makes a wonderful textured print.

Crop photo copy of hair for a textured pattern.

- Photo copy some plant sprigs. Bamboo has an attractive leaf pattern. Try a pine sprig or grasses.

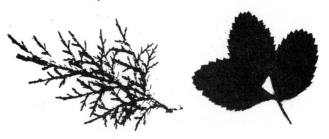

A bit of greenery

- Many rubber stamps can be stamped repeatedly to make a patterned background.
- There are many computer-generated patterns suitable for backgrounds.

LAYERED BACKGROUNDS

A background does not have to be just a backdrop for a second, more dramatic printing. Print the same background a second time in subtle colors.

Rubber stamp textured background

PRINT ONE BACKGROUND OVER ANOTHER

These two textures were made with spongy children's stamps.

- Print the solid squares in red-orange.
- Over this using raspberry red ink, print the squares with holes in the middle. (See MULTICOLOR PRINTING, p. 55.) Raspberry red is equal parts of Red and Fluorescent Purple ink.

First print

Design for second print

Fist and second print combined.

MULTIPLE PRINTINGS OF ONE BACKGROUND

Moiré patterns are made when geometrically regular patterns such as grids or checks are printed over each other. The overlapping of the patterns creates a second pattern. Changing the angle at which the second printing overlaps the first changes the moiré pattern. The moiré effect can be exploited with Gocco printing.

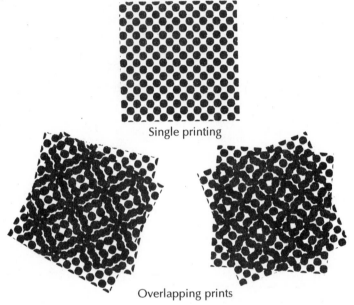

Single printing

Overlapping prints

PLAID

Make irregular stripes with the Gocco Brush Pen. Make two Masters: one with horizontal stripes and one with vertical stripes. Print the horizontals, let them dry, then print the verticals in a different color at right angles over the horizontals. The result will look like loosely woven fabric.

Stripes and plaids

Try printing stripes over each other at odd angles instead of right angles.

"Plaid" variations

COLOR IDEAS

Print subtle color differences such as shades of taupe and gray on ivory paper.

Try one set of stripes in blue and the other in yellow. The intersections of the stripes will be blue green if you print yellow stripes over blue.

APPLICATIONS

Now that you are surrounded with an array of striped and plaid papers, what are you going to do with them? These are two Masters to save and reuse in many ways.

- The picture side of a postcard

- The outside of greeting cards with plaid wrapping around to the back of the card.

Plaid book cover

- Wrapping paper: (See STAMP KIT FOR CLOTH, PRINTING ON OTHER SURFACES, p. 171.)

MASKING REGISTRATION

This is an easy way to make something look as if you have carefully registered it. This technique works on simple objects, something easy to cut around. (This is a popular rubber stamp technique.)

- First print pink hearts on good paper, then print several more on scrap paper.

Printed hearts

- Cut the scrap paper heart s out exactly along the edges.
- Clean Master and reink in red.
- Place cut out heart *precisely* over the now-dry printed pink heart. A dab of Post-A-Note glue on the back of the cut out heart will hold it in place.
- Print red heart so it is partially overlapping the pink one. Remove cut out heart. The pink heart will appear to be partly hidden behind the red one.

Overlapping in two prints

VARIATIONS

FISH SURROUNDED BY WAVES

- First print a fish on good paper, then print several more on scrap paper.
- Carefully cut out the scrap paper fish exactly around the edges.

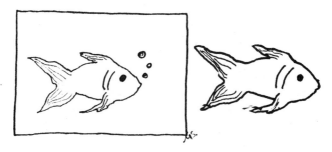

Fish printed on good paper   Cut out fish

- Prepare a Master with a wave background.

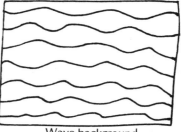

Wave background

- When fish on good paper is dry, carefully place a cut out fish right over it.

- Over this print a wave background.

Wave background printed over fish

- Remove the cut out fish, which now has waves printed on it. The covered up fish will be surrounded by waves.

Fish surrounded by waves

- You will notice a ridge of ink on the Master around the area of the cut out fish. Print on scrap paper to remove the ink build up, so it will not transfer to the next print.

ENVELOPES

Print envelopes to coordinate with the fish/background design.

- Place one of the cut out fish on a blank envelope where the address will go.
- Print the wave background on the envelope. The background will have a fish-shaped "hole" where you can write the address.

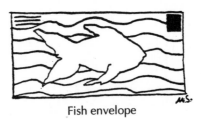

Fish envelope

EXACT REGISTRATION

Some multi-color effects cannot be done in just one printing. To have the colors *exactly* where you want them, separate the design and print each separation on individual Masters. "Separation" means to divide your design by colors. Colors adjacent to each other will be separated; one on one Master, one on another Master. This way the colors will be just where you want them when you print. There may be more than one color on a Master if there is enough room so they can be kept apart with ink block, or if it doesn't matter if they blend together. The techniques presented thus far in this chapter are building blocks to exact registration.

PLANNING YOUR STRATEGY

It is important to think through how to separate the design. What part will be on one Master, what on another. How many Masters will you need? In what order will the printing be done?

Design, Part one

Consider colored letters outlined in black. Even with careful inking, it is not possible to apply ink so an even black outline prints around the colored letters. Separate this design into two components: one for the outline and another for the colored letters. Each component will be on a separate Master. Print letters first; the outline, second. The outline should slightly overlap the letters.

Thermographic embossing could be part of your plan. Picture a shiny black outline around red colored letters. Change the look by using gold embossing powder for the outline and printing the letters in dark blue. (See EMBOSSING, p. 69.)

REGISTER MARKS

HOLD STILL!!!

In preparing your design, exposing the Masters and printing, you want to control everything that moves: paper and Masters. It is important that all papers, both in preparing the design and in printing, be carefully and precisely placed. You do not want anything to move mid-process. The more precise you are in all steps of registration, the more successful you will be and the easier your printing will be

Register marks will help keep papers in place while preparing the separation and when exposing the Masters. A register mark on one paper will line up exactly with a corresponding mark on another paper.

Register marks are available at graphic art stores.

TYPES OF REGISTER MARKS

- Register marks on tape have circles with plus signs over them. Place each mark carefully so a mark on one piece of paper will line up precisely with a mark on another paper.

Example of register marks

- Other register marks separate into two parts. Place mark sticky side down on base paper. Put a paper over the mark and burnish mark. The mark will separate into two interconnected circular symbols: one on the base paper and one on the *back side* of the top paper. The two symbols fit together perfectly so you can always get your papers back in exactly the same position. A limitation of this type of mark is that if you photo copy your work, the mark on the back side is not copied.

POSITIONING REGISTER MARKS

Practice lining up register marks on tracing paper.

- Place one mark in a bottom corner of your paper so it is like a plus sign (+) and another mark in the diagonally opposite upper corner so it is like an x.

- Each part of the separated design will have a pair of marks on it that line up with marks on a plain base sheet.

- The base sheet has only the register marks on it, no design. The base sheet will go on the Foam Base of the Printer as a guide for placing each part of the design when you expose the Masters.

Position of register marks

LIGHT TABLE

A light table is helpful, nearly essential. Make an improvised light table by propping up a sheet of clear Plexiglas and placing a light under it. Use a window if you don't mind working vertically.

PREPARING THE SEPARATION

- Cut plain white paper larger than the Foam Base, so register marks are outside the printing area. Cut paper 5" x 7" or larger for the B6; 7" x 10" for the B5. Cut extras.

- Tape part #1 with HAPPY BIRTHDAY to your light table. Put register marks in opposite corners. This is your *guide* for preparing components of the separation. You will *not* use this to expose a Master.

- Tape paper #2 over part #1. Place register marks on #2 so they line up with the marks on part #1. Draw in the filling for the letters. Be careful to take filling to just inside the edges of the letters. When printing, the outline of the letters will overlap the fill a bit. This makes registration easier

Design part two

- Remove part #2 with completed filling of HAPPY BIRTHDAY and set it aside.

Design part three

- Place paper #3 over part #1. Draw the outline of the letters of HAPPY BIRTHDAY. Do not make the outline pencil thin: registration will be easier if the outline is a little thicker.

NOTES

- Do not stack up layers of papers on sheet #1 as you prepare the separations: This can distort your work. Remove each sheet when you finish that part of the design.

- If you did your separations on tracing paper, photo copy them, because tracing paper often has a slight gloss and the Master will not expose well. (See PREPARING DESIGNS, SHINY SURFACES, p. 36.)

- If you photo copy your work, copy *every* component of the design. Copy machines can change a design just slightly, enough to distort your carefully done registration. Be sure to make extra copies, just in case.

- Note: Many computer graphic programs will print out separated designs with register dots in place, ready for printing.

EXPOSING THE MASTERS

PRINT MASTERS

There is some leeway in how Masters fit in the Printer, especially in the older orange and yellow models of the B6. To compensate for this, nudge each Master down and to the left as far as it will go. Try to get the same feel each time you put in a Master.

EXPOSING MASTERS

- Using your light table, put down part # 3, the letter fillings. Put repositionable glue stick in two or three places outside of design area.

- Carefully place part #2 over part #3, lining up register marks.

Parts two and part three of design

- Put two or three dots of glue stick on paper.
- Put two strips of double stick tape across foam pad of Printer.
- Securely press stack of papers onto pad.
- Expose first Master with design part 3 which is on the top of the stack.
- As you raise the Printer lid up, be careful that paper #3 stays attached to the Master rather than the base. This makes inking the Master easier. Check that the first Master is well exposed before exposing the next one.

SECURING THE MASTERS

When you put the inked Masters back in the Printer, try to position them in the same way you did for exposing. If there is any looseness at all in how the Master fits, tape it to the body of the Printer.

- With the B6 put two pieces of Masking tape diagonally across the upper corners of the Master.

Tape securing Master to Printer

- For the B5 put a strip of tape on the two ends of the Master.
- If you have to reink the Master, put it back the same way. Keep the copies you made after reinking separate from the first copies, as the alignment may have changed. You may have to make an adjustment in paper position for the second print of the reinked copies.

PRINTING

FIRST PRINTING

When doing the first printing, it is important to position each paper in exactly the same place on the Foam Base, so the second printing will be easy to line up. A positioning "L" or screen printing tabs are invaluable here. (Review REGISTRATION, PRECISE PAPER PLACEMENT. p. 119)

- Cut several pieces of test paper the same size as your good paper.
- Attach to the Foam Base the Mylar overlay you made in ALIGNMENT. Turn the Mylar sheet out of the way to the left.
- Ink master from part #2, the "filling" of the letters.
- Print this image on the base.

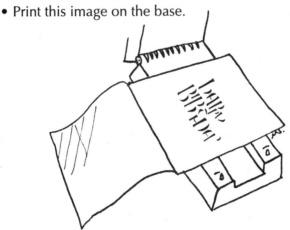

Mylar overlay with image printed on base

- Determine where to place printing paper on base. Use an "L" or tabs on base to hold each paper in the same place.
- Print several scrap papers the same size as your good paper, and then your good paper.
- Be aware that paper with a deckled edge is difficult to line up, because the edge is not sharp and even. Align paper along edges that are not deckled. As a

last resort you may, gasp, have to cut off the deckled edge!

SECOND PRINTING

- Ink Master 2, the letter outline, and put it in Printer. Turn Mylar back over base, i.e., close the book.

Print outline image on Mylar.

- The outline letters on the Mylar should line up with the filled letters printed on the base from first printing. If they do, you are in luck; proceed with the second printing using the same paper guides used for first printing.

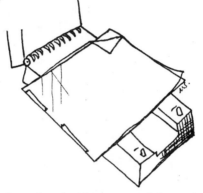

Mylar sheet closed with Happy Birthday outline on it

- Is it a bit off? Use the Mylar to help adjust the paper guides. Slide one of your first printings on test paper under Mylar. Hold Mylar in place with one hand and use your other hand to adjust paper under the Mylar. Line up image on paper with image on the Mylar.

- When you have the paper in position, hold it in place and turn Mylar back to the left.

- Adjust printing guides so they hold paper in its new position. Print a test sheet. Once printing guides are readjusted for the second printing, place each paper along guides and print away.

- Use Master Cleaner or Goop to remove printed image from Mylar if you want to start over.

THOUGHTS ON USING THE MYLAR OVERLAY

Once you use a Mylar overlay, you will see how easy registered printing is. You may wonder why you should bother with a positioning "L" or masking tape tabs, and choose to work with just a Mylar overlay.

However, if you do much registered printing, you will find that using either the tabs or an "L" will save much time. Without tabs or an "L" you will have to align each paper carefully under the Mylar before you print. This is time-consuming.

ALTERNATE METHODS OF SEPARATING A DESIGN

DRAWN SEPARATIONS

The preceding instructions for HAPPY BIRTHDAY used the method of drawing, or tracing, each component of the design separation. The advantage of this method is that you can prepare the separations so there is a tiny overlap of the components of the design. In this case, the outline of the letters overlapped the fill. This makes registration easier and assures you that there will not be a sliver of blank paper showing between the outline of the letters and the fill.

CUT APART SEPARATIONS

Designs that are *not* continuous can be cut apart and printed separately.

The letters ABCXYZ are too close together to keep the colors apart, and there is no room to use Ink Block to contain the colors.

Design for separation

• Cut into two parts: AYC and BXZ.

- Be sure to make extra photo copies so you will have emergency replacements.

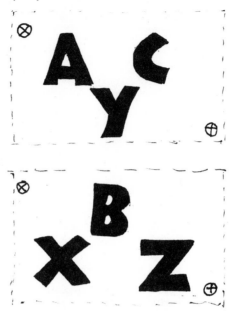

Design cut in to two parts

- In working with cut portions of a design, glue down the parts for each separate printing and position them just as you would if you were tracing or drawing them in the HAPPY BIRTHDAY example.
- Use register marks to keep the parts aligned.
- Print AYC and BXZ with separate Masters and in different colors.

ALMOST REGISTRATION

This is a forgiving variation of exact registration with the same motto as in life: give yourself a little slack! The process is the same as for exact registration. The difference is in making a design that allows a little leeway without looking like a mistake.

If you aren't sure you would like to try exact registration, try this for great results.

- Start with boldly outlined letters for a pattern.

Outline letters

- Using a light table, put rough finish paper over the outlined letters. With a crayon make rough strokes over the letters to "color" them in, but don't color just inside the lines! The effectiveness of this technique is going outside the lines for a spontaneous look...and to give you some slack!

"Colored in" letters

- Print using the same steps used in printing HAPPY BIRTHDAY.

- Print the "crayon" coloring first in bright colors.

- Print the outline in black over the "crayon" coloring.

Finished design

PROCESS COLOR PRINTING

Use the Gocco process color inks, Cyan, Magenta, and Yellow.

- Prepare your own color separations using a computer.
  - ◆ Scan in your own color photo or picture.
  - ◆ Use a graphic software program to separate the colors for CMYK printing.
  - ◆ Note: The Gocco Process Color set includes only Cyan, Magenta, and Yellow. Black, signified as K is the fourth color. It adds emphasis and shadows.

Cyan

Magenta

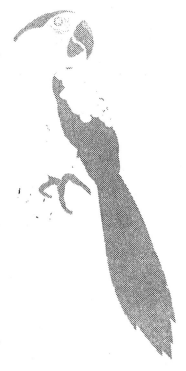

Yellow

- Print each part in the correct sequence, starting with Cyan, *then*, Magenta, *then*, Yellow.

POSSIBILITIES

As you do more multiple printing, you will readily see many possibilities. As in everything else, the more you do, the more ideas will flow, *and* the easier it becomes!

Print this tree in two shades of green, one part in medium the other in dark. Print the stars last. Use gold embossing to emphasize the stars.

Note: Be sure the green ink is *thoroughly* dry before printing and embossing the stars. Embossing powder easily adheres to ink that is partially dry.

First print in dark green

Second print in medium green

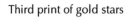

★ MERRY CHRISTMAS ★

Third print of gold stars

★ MERRY CHRISTMAS ★

Finished print

B6 STAMP KIT FOR CLOTH

CONTENTS

PREPARING THE MASTER

PRINTING

FABRIC

PRINTING SURFACE

REGISTRATION

CLEAN UP

CARE OF PRINTED ITEMS

MIXED MEDIA ON FABRIC

PRINTING ON OTHER SURFACES

POSSIBILITIES

B6 STAMP KIT FOR CLOTH

This is an exciting accessory for the B6 Gocco Printer! It is the easiest way to print, not only on fabric, but also on large pieces of paper...even wallpaper! Think of the Stamper as a portable printer. It can print on just about anything that will stay still. Use like a giant rubber stamp that does not need reinking after each stamping.

It will print on items that are too large or bulky to fit in the printer, e.g., sweat shirts and sweat pants. A versatile feature is that a Master can be used with cloth ink, then cleaned and reinked with High Mesh ink and used to print on paper. This allows you to expand a theme, printing the same image on shirts, aprons, invitations, napkins, paper or cloth table cloths, shopping bags, etc.

CONTENTS

- A foam pad of a softer foam, but the same size as the Foam Base of the B6 Printer. On top of the pad is a large easy-to-hold handle. A piece of clear Mylar on the bottom of the pad protects the pad's sticky base. Discard the one inch wide band around the sides of the foam pad.
- Four tubes, 40 cc each, of water-based Stamp Ink for Cloth: Black, Red, Blue, Yellow. Green, Brown and White ink are available separately.
- Ink Block
- Two pieces of adhesive board to stabilize the fabric. Adhesive boards are similar to photograph albums page with a Mylar protector over a tacky sheet.
- Four "C"-shaped supports for the stamp pad to rest on. These also help separate the just-printed fabric from the Master when pulling the stamper away from the fabric.
- Instructions and some clip art.

PREPARING THE MASTER

Stock up on Masters and bulbs; they are not included in the Kit. Expose Master in Printer as usual.

INKING THE MASTER

Since the Stamp Ink for Cloth is a water-based ink, it will dry quickly and clog the Master. Have everything prepared to print before inking the Master! (This is different from the oil-water emulsion High Mesh Inks which do not readily dry in the Master.) Do not remove original design from Master except to check that the Master exposed properly. Take original off Master after inking just before printing. This keeps ink from drying in Master.

Use Ink Block to separate colors whenever possible. Cloth Ink is not as thick as High Mesh Ink. This means that the colors will spread and mix more easily than High Mesh inks. Colors can be mixed, but do not mix water-based Cloth Ink with the oil-base High Mesh Ink. Oil and water do not mix!

Apply a generous amount of ink. Cloth ink does not go as far as High Mesh ink. However, do not use so much ink that it will ooze out the sides of the Master. It is better to reink more frequently.

TYPES OF INK

The Gocco Stamp Ink for Cloth is made specifically for the Cloth Stamper. Non-Gocco textile inks made for screen printing and fabric painting have a thinner consistency than Gocco Cloth Ink. Because they are thinner, too much ink will pass through the Master making a smudged image.

SECURE MYLAR TOP SHEET

After inking the Master, replace Mylar top sheet over the Master. The ink will hold the Master and Mylar cover sheet together for medium to large images.

With a small design there may not be enough ink to hold the Master together. The Mylar may slip to one side. Securing it with tape or paper clips with prevent this. Slip a paper clip on both sides of the open end of the Master to secure Mylar to the cardboard frame of the Master. You could also use masking tape.

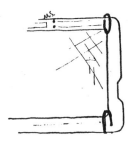

Secure Mylar sheet to Master with paper clips.

PRINTING

THE TACKY BASE OF THE STAMPER

A clear protective sheet covers the base of the Stamper. Carefully remove this before printing and put it aside where it will not be lost. When you are finished, put sheet back on the base to protect its tacky surface. Eventually the base will loose its tackiness, but can easily be rejuvenated:

- Carefully run water over just the tacky surface, not the foam, and let air dry.
- Or press masking or clear tape, sticky side to the base, and lift up. Repeat several times.

ATTACHING MASTER

Is everything ready? Place inked Master, printing side down, Mylar side up, on work surface. Put Foam Base of Stamper carefully on the Mylar in the middle of the cardboard frame. The Stamper base is very sticky and will adhere readily to the Mylar. Now remove original from Master.

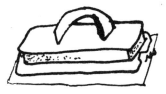

Placing Stamper on B-6 Print Master

PRINTING PRESSURE

To print, stamp down firmly until you feel the pad meeting the resistance of the table. Practice printing on the same, or at least similar, fabric as that in your project.

Stamping on fabric has a different feel from stamping on paper.

Be careful to stamp down squarely, and to exert firm, even pressure on the entire printing area. Using too much pressure or pumping up and down will cause a smudged image.

CLOGGED MASTER

Whenever you pause printing, cover Master with a piece of wax paper or plastic wrap to prevent ink from drying and clogging the Master.

If the Master will not print and is well inked, the Master is probably clogged. Wipe the outside of the printing surface of the Master with wet paper toweling to soften dried ink. Dry Master, make a few prints on a scrap to get the smudges off, and resume printing.

If the ink has dried thoroughly, even scrubbing will not unclog the Master. Start over with a new Master!

REINKING

You will get 15 to 20 prints before you need to reink, depending on the design density and amount of ink used. Printing on fabric will not make as many copies as printing on paper. Watch your printing very closely for the first sign of ink running out. Stop immediately and reink. Do not try to do just one more print.

Loosen the paper clips holding the Mylar to Master, but do not remove Mylar from the stamper. Instead pull the bottom of the Master away from the Mylar...like opening a book. Prop the open Master and Stamper on the table and reink.

Inking Master while it is attached to Stamp Pad

The ink may have pulled over the ink block. If you used several colors but no ink block, you will see considerable movement of the colors. In either case, you may be able to use a spatula to move some of the colors back where you want them. If the colors are smeared, pull Mylar away from Stamper pad, clean the Master and reink it.

FABRIC

TYPES

The Gocco Cloth Ink works best on 100% cotton or cotton polyester blends. Smooth fabrics show fine details best. Details blur on textured surfaces such as terry cloth and corduroy. Avoid nylon. Most nylon has a water repellent coating to which the ink will not bond.

Before beginning an important project, do some tests printing, heat setting, and washing the fabric. Use a permanent marker to make notes directly on your test pieces.

PREPARATION

Many fabrics are treated with sizing, like starch. It is best to launder first to remove the sizing so ink can penetrate into the fibers

PRINTING SURFACE

A smooth flat surface is important. This includes smoothing out wrinkles in the fabric!

Holding down the fabric is also important. Fabric will cling to the Master when the Stamp Pad is lifted up from the fabric. This can cause the wet ink to smear. It also moves the fabric, which means you have to restraighten the fabric if you are doing more than one print.

"C"-SHAPED SUPPORTS

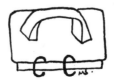

"C" shaped supports on Stamp Pad

The four "C" shaped supports that come with the Stamp Kit snap on to the Stamper, two on each side of the Stamper.

They are meant to help release fabric from the Stamper after making a print , but they tend to splay out and to get in the way. They also can smear wet ink from an adjacent print when doing multiple prints near each other.

ADHESIVE BOARDS

The best way to hold fabric in place for printing is to place it on a tacky surface.

STAMP KIT ADHESIVE BOARD

The two adhesive boards that comes with the Stamper work well for single printings, but at $5^1/_2$" x 9" they are too small for repeat prints.

Larger boards, $8^1/_4$" x $11^3/_4$", are available from Gocco dealers. To hold board in place remove protective Mylar sheets from *both* sides of board; one side of board will adhere to work surface and the other to the fabric. When board is not in use, replace the protective sheets. Eventually the board will loose its stickiness. Note: These adhesive boards are similar to popular photo album pages. Perhaps you have some extra album pages.

LARGE ADHESIVE BOARD

For large items involving multiple printing, use a large piece of smooth cardboard or foam core board. Lightly coat the board with spray adhesive. (Scotch Spray Mount or 3M Spray Adhesive) Let adhesive dry a few minutes so it feels tacky. Spread fabric smoothly over board and print away! Spray board again when it looses its tackiness.

If the board is larger that the fabric, you can make guide marks on the board to help align printing, e.g., for a border around a scarf. When printing several items, prepare several boards so each piece can dry undisturbed. Once everything is ready, printing will go quickly.

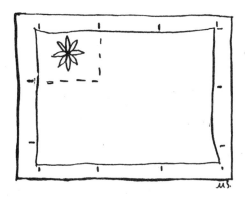

Dotted lines indicate area of first printing

SMALL ADHESIVE BACKING

For smaller items, spray a piece of card stock or manila file folder. Tape this to your work surface to secure it for printing.

MASKING TAPE

Fabric can also be taped to a smooth work surface. Run masking tape around the item's perimeter. This is best for a very large piece, e.g., a table cloth, sheet or yard goods, but is a nuisance if you are printing many items.

TEE SHIRTS

Be sure to place a board inside a T shirt. Ink can go right through the front of the shirt and onto the back.

To print on sleeves, cut a board the length and width of the sleeve, and slide inside the sleeve. This will give a smooth surface so you are not printing over the ridge of the sleeve seam.

REGISTRATION

Registration with the Cloth Stamper is a bit different from the methods discussed in the REGISTRATION CHAPTER, p. 113.

WHICH WAY IS UP?

Once the Master is attached to the Stamper, there is no way of telling which is the top of your design from looking at the Stamper handle. This can mean trouble. It is very easy to pick up the Stamper, stamp away, and realize *after* you have printed that the design is upside down! Put a piece of masking tape on top of the Stamper and draw a bold arrow on the tape pointing to the top of the design.

Arrow on Stamper to indicate top of design

PLACEMENT GUIDES ON FABRIC

PENS

Disappearing fabric marking pens are an excellent way to mark guides on fabric. There are two kinds: one sponges out with a cloth dampened in cold water; the other fades away in a day or two. The fading pen saves time, providing you finish the project before your marks vanish!

TAPE

Masking tape is another easy way to mark fabric. An advantage of tape is that you can also make guide lines and notes on the tape. The edge of tape is more precise for exact placement than is a drawn guide line.

GUIDE SHEETS

Guide sheets can help you visualize ahead of time how the printed image will look on your garment and how to position the image.

- Cut sheets of tracing paper or Mylar $7^1/_2''$ x $5^5/_8''$, the outside dimensions of a B6 Master. (Mylar can be wiped off and reused.) Cut extra guide sheets; they are a staple of fabric stamping. Store them in an envelope with your Stamper.

- With inked Master attached to Stamper, carefully place Master on a guide sheet, lining up edges of Master with edges of guide sheet. Print. Remove printed guide sheet from Master. Careful, do not smear the wet ink or get it on your clean fingers.

- Place printed guide sheet on garment to determine the best placement.

Possible placement of designs before printing

- Using masking tape or fading fabric markers, mark on garment at least two corners of the guide sheet.

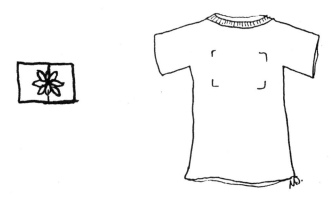

Marks indication where to place Master for printing

- Remove guide sheet from garment.
- To print, carefully place Master within the corner marks. The image will print where you planned... no rude surprises.
- Be sure to print your design right side up! Remember the arrow on Stamp Pad.

TO CENTER A DESIGN ON A SHIRT

- Draw a vertical line through center of image printed on guide sheet. Folding design in half is a quick way to find the center.

Mark center of design

- Find center of shirt by folding shirt in half lengthwise. Mark center line. Place shirt flat again.

Center line on shirt

- Place guide sheet on shirt, lining up center line on guide sheet with center line on shirt.

Guide sheet on center of shirt

• Mark the corners of guide sheet on shirt.

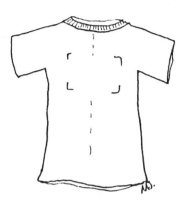

Marks indicating corners of guide sheet

BORDER PRINTING

Printing a border is easy. There are many items that are perfect for borders: skirts, waistbands, long sleeves, collars, cuffs, scarves, sweat pants, curtains, tablecloths, place mats, pillow cases, sheets, banners, ad infinitum.

- Print several guide sheets, depending on size of project.
- Place guide sheets on garment, adjusting spacing between sheets. Generally, you will want an equal amount of space between each image.

Guide sheets on garment

- If you are printing a border that is to have an equal margin at the left and right end of the fabric, plan this *before* you start printing. This is not difficult, it just takes foresight.

- On the fabric draw a base line for the border along the bottom of the guide sheets. You can also use the edge of the fabric, depending on where you want the image to print.

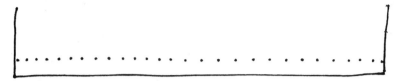

Dotted base line on fabric

- Mark the left sides of two or three guide sheets with a small mark perpendicular to the base line. These are the left corner marks for placing the Master. Measure the space between these lines. This is the repeat interval. Continue marking the repeat interval to the right end of border.

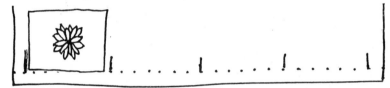

Marks of repeat interval indicating Master placement

- For each printing place Master with its lower left corner at each left corner mark on fabric and bottom of Master along the base line.

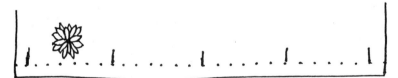

First print of border

- If the repeat intervals are close together, the Master may overlap part of a fresh print just made. The wet ink will transfer to the Master, and then to the fabric with the next print producing a light ghost image. To avoid this, print every other, or even every third image. Since you have already marked your guide lines, you will have no problem printing every other image. When the first printings are dry, go back and print the in-between images.

Print every other image

• Note: In a hurry for the ink to dry? Use a hair dryer.

BORDER VARIATIONS

VARIED FLOWERS
Maybe you want more than one kind or color of flower. Print every other flower with a daisy. Change to a pansy Master to print between each daisy.

GARLAND
By making the base line wavy, a straight floral border will change into a free flowing garland. Draw a wavy line for guide or just work with a "line" in your head, and estimate the intervals.

Single garland

Double garland on both sides of base line

STRIPES

Make "stripes" of repeated borders printed parallel to each other. Try alternating stripes of a flower border and a leaf border.

Floral and leaf stripes

ALL OVER PRINTING

The Stamper is so simple to use that it is easy to do repeat prints for an all-over effect on a large area, e.g., scarves, skirts, curtains, and sheets, and yards of fabric before cutting and sewing.

REPEATS

Plan a pattern along a grid or at random.

- One plan is a checkerboard grid with a print made in each square. Use a fabric marker to make grid lines.

Patterns based on a grid

- For a random pattern to look good, there still needs to be some regularity so it does not look uneven. Look at the overall effect as you are stamping.

MASKING REGISTRATION

To make one image appear in front of and slightly overlapping another image use masking registration (See REGISTRATION, MASKING REGISTRATION, p. 134.) It works the same on fabric as on paper. This can add a new look to your stamping.

EXACT REGISTRATION

- See REGISTRATION, EXACT REGISTRATION, p. 136 for information on separating a design for two or more printings, and exposing Masters.

- Print the first part of design on fabric. Allow to dry.

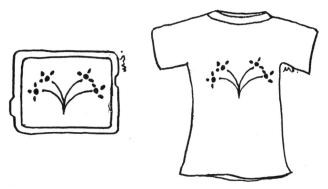

Print first part of design on a shirt

- Make the second part of design on a guide sheet, placing Master exactly over guide sheet. Remove guide sheet from Master.

- Place guide sheet with second image over first printing on fabric. Adjust position of guide sheet over first image. Use masking tape to mark the edges of guide sheet. Masking tape is more precise than fabric markers.

Second part of design

- Remove guide sheet. Place Print Master exactly along masking tape lines and print.

Finished shirt

CLEAN UP

Because cloth ink dries quickly in the Master, it is not a good idea to store an inked Master. When you finish printing, clean Master immediately.

- Remove Master from Stamper. Lift up Mylar sheet and scrape ink off Mylar and Master with a spatula. Wipe off Master and Mylar with damp paper toweling. Spray Master with Windex to remove last vestige of ink, and wipe dry. It is important to remove all ink from Master. A residue of ink will dry and *permanently* clog Master.

- It is tempting to wash the Master in running water. Don't! The cardboard frame shrinks when it gets wet and will not keep the Master taut for the next use.
- Remember, this is water base ink, so do *not* use Master Cleaner or Goop!
- Save ink in an airtight container or Ink Cone for reuse.

CARE OF PRINTED ITEMS

HEAT SET

It is imperative that printed items be heat set before washing. Let print dry completely. If you are in a hurry, use a hair dryer. Cover image with a piece of paper or a light pressing cloth. Set iron at correct setting for fabric. Iron for two minutes on front and back. Do not leave iron in just one spot for two minutes or fabric will scorch!

A home clothes dryer does not get hot enough to set the ink. Some commercial dryers are hotter, but do a test first.

LAUNDERING

Fabric may be machine washed on a short to medium cycle with mild soap and warm water. Do not bleach or wash in hot water. Dry in clothes dryer or drip dry. Do not dry clean.

MIXED MEDIA ON FABRIC

These "visual hints" are equally suitable for images printed with the Screen Kit for Cloth as with the PG Kit.

OUTLINING

A time-saving and creative use of the Stamping Kit For Cloth or a PG Master is to print a detailed line drawing of a design, perhaps a flower, on a T-shirt. Use the printed image as a guide to embellish the flower with paints, dyes, fabric appliques, etc. Each shirt will be unique, but with out the work of hand-drawing the design every time.

FABRIC PENS, DYES AND PAINTS

Fabric inks such as glitter paints, slick paints, puff paints, and fabric marking pens can add to your Gocco-printed design. One idea leads to another. Here are a few starters:

- Shade in the printed outline of the flower with several colors of fabric marking pens.
- Use fabric dyes to color another flower. Dyes are free flowing and will give a water color effect to the flower.
- Paint in a flower with iridescent fabric paints which are more opaque than fabric pens or dyes for yet another variation.

DIMENSIONAL FABRIC PAINTS

- Print a red heart. Add a purple slick paint outline, or draw an arrow through a heart with silver glitter paint.

- Print watermelon slices. Add shiny black seeds with slick paint.

- Stamp a row of pumpkins. Use a green slick paint or a fabric marking pen to draw vines and tendrils to connect the pumpkins.

- Make a Master with a cluster of holly leaves. After heat setting the ink, add shiny red holly berries using red slick paint. (Slick paints do not need heat setting and will melt when ironed. Note: Check heat setting and laundering instructions of all inks, dyes and paints.

- Print several evergreen trees. Add white puff paint, heat according to directions and you will have snow-ladened branches. Note: If you are adding puff paint to a screen printed image, heat set the image *before* adding the puff paint.
  Add "frost" to the tree with silver or iridescent glitter paint.
  Draw a star on the tree top with silver or gold glitter paint, or glue on a sequin star.

- Print a border of gingerbread men "cookies" around an apron and on matching towels. Use white slick paint to add a frosting outline and black puff paint for raisin eyes and buttons.

- Note: Many dimensional paints do not need to be heat set and, moreover, will melt if ironed, making a terrible mess. Be sure to heat set your Gocco print *before* adding dimensional paints!

OTHER FABRIC "ADD ONS"

- Make a Master of a small fir branch. Use the Fabric Stamper to do repeat stampings to shape a large evergreen "tree" on the front of a sweat shirt. From the inside of the shirt, pin on small painted wooden ornaments to trim the tree. Finish off the wreath by attaching a red bow. Pinning the bow on makes removal easy at laundry time.

- Add lace or ribbon bows to a bouquet or garland of flowers done with the Stamper.

- Enliven a stamped teddy bear with glued on "eyes" and a ribbon around his neck.

- Visit fabric and craft stores to find sequins, rhinestones, ribbons and many other items to combine with your Gocco projects. As with everything else in life, the more you do this, the more ideas you'll get.

- Note: Test the washability of "add ons" before laundering.

PRINTING ON OTHER SURFACES

PAPER

Use the Stamper to print any paper too large to fit in the Printer. Ink Master with High Mesh ink and stamp the same as fabric, adjusting pressure.

- Shelf or banner paper quickly becomes paper table cloths for a large party, picnic, or family reunion.

- Large shopping bags

- Wallpaper

- Brown kraft paper in green or brown. Tie package with green or tan jute garden twine.

- Coordinate wrapping paper, tissue paper, and even ribbon.

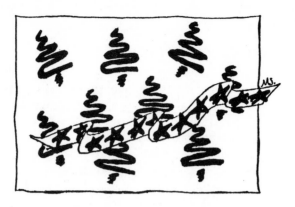

Wrapping paper and matching ribbon

HARD SURFACES

These items do not print well in the Printer. They are so rigid that they absorb the resilience of the foam pad that pushes up against the Master to help squeeze out the ink. Printing with the Stamper remedies this, since the Stamper's foam base is on *top* of the Master.

- Print boxes and box lids.

- Coordinate floors with walls.

- Print cutting guides for woodwork and model-making.

- Stamp on wood plaques, mat board.

- Walls, yes, walls! Picture a "stencil" border that coordinates with upholstery or drapery fabric.

Printing border around window

POSSIBILITIES

Possibilities of fabric printing seem endless.

CLOTHING

Almost any article of clothing can be printed.

- Print company logos on a shirt.

- Print a team name down the sleeve or leg of a sweat suit, on the back of a jacket, on shorts, or golf shirts.

- Personalize clothing with an initial or monogram, small and subtle on a cuff or bold on the back or front of a shirt.

- Shirts, sweat pants, shorts, scarves, socks, aprons. Print fish on shirt, then draw in fishing line with a fabric marker.

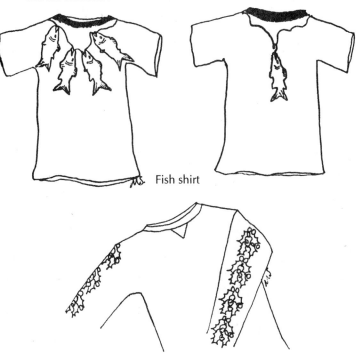

Fish shirt

Holly garlands on shirt

- Print a string of lights on an apron. Make a Master with four bulbs. Repeat printing the same as a flower border. See page 166. When finished, draw in the cord with a fabric marking pen.

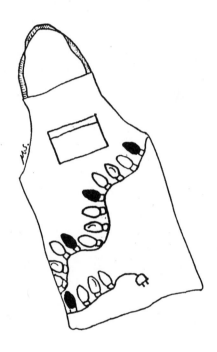

Apron with string of lights

- Personalize children's clothes, baby gifts.
- Print laundry tags for clothing.
- Make tags for hand made garments.
- Print precise cutting guides for quilt patterns.

- Embellish tote bags. Print three images on tote bag: bucket, ball, and shovel using MASKING REGISTRATION, p. 134.

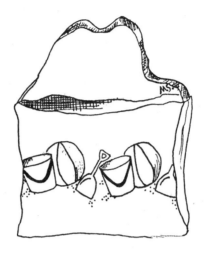

Tote bag with several images

LINENS AND HOME DECOR

- For a country-style room, picture what could be done with a profusion of assorted summer flowers printed on pillows and linens.

Printed pillows

- Pillow cases and sheets can be printed all over or with just a border on the hem.

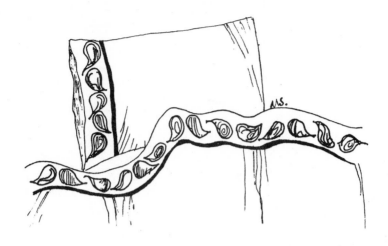

Border on sheet and pillow

- In the kitchen, print vegetables and herbs.
- Coordinate aprons, linen or cotton dish towels, hot pads, curtains, place mats, tablecloths, napkins.
- For a child's room, teddy bears, balloons and clouds could drift across walls and even ceiling.
- Baby shower? Print bibs, crib sheets, clothing, canvas tote bags.
- Wedding shower gifts? Delight the bride with personalized cotton or linen dish towels. Print the bride and groom's initials and their wedding date.

Wear and display your projects with pride!

SCREEN KIT PG

CONTENTS

THE GENERAL IDEA

EXPOSING PG MASTERS

TEXTILE INKS

SQUEEGEE HINTS

PRINTING

COLOR EFFECTS

USING PRINT MASTERS

REGISTRATION

CLEAN UP

CARE OF PRINTED ITEMS

POSSIBILITIES

SCREEN KIT PG

The PG Kit (that's "PG" as in Print Gocco) is a quick easy introduction to screen printing with a squeegee. Use your B6 Printer to expose PG Masters, and print with a squeegee. PG Masters are included in the PG Kit and are available separately.

CONTENTS

- 2 PG 701 Masters
- 2 PG 702 Masters
- 4 Textile Inks: Black, Red, Blue, Yellow, 50 cc ea.
- Medium Riso Pen
- 2 Plastic Squeegees: 4″ and 5^{13}/$_{16}$″ wide
- Correction Fluid
- Red Filter
- Clip art
- Instructions

THE GENERAL IDEA

Use the B6 Gocco Printer to expose the PG Masters; printing is done with a squeegee. PG 701 Master is the same size as a B6 Master, and is exposed in one flashing. PG 702 is roughly the size of two B6 Masters placed side-by-side, and is exposed in two flashings. Flashed areas overlap slightly. Prepare original the same way as when exposing Print Masters. Be sure to have extra bulbs; they are not included in the Kit.

The ease of PG Masters is that the Screen Master is mounted to a frame ready to expose and print. The same Screen Master is also available in sheets or by the roll from some Gocco dealers. PG Masters resemble Print Masters, but they do not have a Mylar top sheet to cover the ink. Printing is done with a squeegee.

PG Masters are made of 70 mesh Screen Master. Remember that High Mesh Print Masters are made of 200 Mesh; finer than the PG Masters. The 70 mesh has two advantages:

- The larger holes allow a heavier deposit of ink, giving excellent coverage on fabric.

- Some pearlescent, luminescent, and very opaque white inks have pigment particles that are too large to pass through High Mesh Print Masters, but will easily go through the 70 mesh.

Check the Yellow Pages for local art and craft stores and screen printing supply shops, also see APPENDIX, SUPPLIES, p. 242.

Avoid inks that do not clean up with water or mineral spirits. Some inks contain strong solvents such as acetones, ketones or lacquer thinner that will dissolve the Master. An example is the ink used to print on nylon fabric used for wind breakers and wind socks.

EXPOSING PG MASTERS

FILTERS

Instructions with PG Masters advise always using a Red Filter when exposing PG Masters to minimize pin dots. If the original is a photo copy, use a Red Filter *and* a Blue Filter. (Many who work with Screen Master do not use a Red Filter and use only the Blue Filter with photo copies.)

IMAGE AREA FOR PG 701

Even though the 701 is the same size as a B6 Master, the image area is smaller to allow room for placing the ink on the Master, the ink reservoir, and to start and stop the squeegee. Pull the squeegee lengthwise or crosswise across the Master. The shape of your design and the width of your squeegee will determine which way you will print.

- Pulling the squeegee from end to end, holding the PG Master vertically, the maximum image area is 4" wide x $4^5/_8$" long.

- Pulling the squeegee from side to side, PG Master horizontal, the maximum image is $5^3/_4$" wide x $2^3/_4$" long.

EXPOSING PG 701

Put PG Master in Printer the same as a Print Master. The notch at the bottom of the PG Master is offset, so the Master will only go in one way. The shiny side of Master will face you. When the top of the Printer is lowered on to the original, this shiny side will be touching the original.

Center design on PG Master, so there is enough margin around the design for ink reservoirs.

IMAGE AREA FOR PG 702

- Master held vertically: image area is $5^3/_4''$ wide x 8" long

- Master held horizontally: image area is 8" wide but only $4^1/_2''$ high. Printing horizontally does not yield any size benefit, because the image area is not any wider, and the height is *less*.

EXPOSING PG 702

Since the 702 Master is wide, part of it will extend to the right of the Gocco Printer for the first flashing, then to the left of Printer for the second flashing. There are two important things to note when exposing a 702 Master.

- Be careful how you put the PG Master in the Printer. It is possible to put the Master in backwards! Place Master so the *shiny side is facing you.* This is the side that must be next to the design when the bulbs flash.

- Position design on PG Master so entire design will be exposed by the two flashings. It is easy to place the design too far to one end of the Master, so part of design extends past the flash area.

    ♦ Holding Master with shiny side facing you and notches on bottom, allow at least $1^1/_4''$ margin on the left end and 1" on the right end.

    ♦ Try a practice run. Lightly tape original facing the shiny side of Master. Place Master first in one set of notches, then in other. Check to be sure all of the design will be exposed by the two flashings. Leave original taped to Master to expose. (Drafting masking tape is not as sticky as regular masking tape and less apt to damage Master when removed.)

- Notches on the Master are placed so there is a $5/_8''$ strip in the center of the Master where areas of the two flashings overlap. Double flashing does not harm the Master and ensures that the design is continuous.

PG 702 Master in B-6 Printer

- After the first flashing, the exposed half of the original will adhere to Master. The exposed area of the image will be a darker black than the unexposed part. Move Master to the next set of notches and expose second half.
- Carefully remove tape and original from Master.

TEXTILE INKS

There are many brands of water-based textile inks that work well with PG Masters in addition to the inks included with the Screen Kit PG. The array of colors is tempting.

Some of the tiny bottles of textile painting inks are suitable as screen printing inks, but are uneconomical, because screen printing needs larger quantities, but beware that many are acrylics that dry so rapidly that they will permanently clog the screen. Look for screen printing or silk screen inks.

Before launching into an important project remember to test print and launder samples!

SUITABLE FABRICS

Water-based inks work best on cotton and cotton polyester blends. They are also suitable for some silks, especially raw silk. Inks, unlike dyes, will change the feel of the fabric, stiffening it a little. This will be most noticeable on soft light weight fabrics.

Avoid nylon fabric. Nylon requires a strong solvent-base ink to bond to the fabric. The solvent, however, will dissolve the Master!

GOCCO STAMP INK FOR CLOTH

This ink is made specifically for the Cloth Stamper. It is thicker than inks made for screen printing, but it can be used to print with a squeegee on PG Masters. Conversely, screen printing inks can *not* be used with the Stamper, because they are too thin to print a crisp image.

PG KIT TEXTILE INK

The jars of red, blue, black, and yellow textile ink included in the Screen Kit PG kit are typical water-based screen printing inks. The PG inks are too thin to use with the Cloth Stamper. Other water-based screen printing inks are also suitable for use with the PG Masters.

PEARLESCENT AND LUMINESCENT INKS

These inks are available in pretty shimmery colors. Their pearly sheen is more pronounced on smooth, tightly woven fabrics rather than rough or nubby fabric.

The pigment particles that make these inks luminescent are often too large to pass through the holes of High Mesh Print Masters, but they will work well with the PG Masters. (Don't confuse these inks with the Gocco High Mesh Pearlescent and Metallic inks, which are not intended for use on fabric.)

WHITE INK

Selecting a white ink requires special attention. Commercial screen printing supply companies are a source for good opaque white inks. A quart will probably be the smallest quantity available. The particles of pigment that make a white very opaque will also cause it to clog in the High Mesh Masters, but will pass through the larger holes of the PG Masters.

Many brands of textile inks sold in art or craft stores have good colors, but poor opaque whites. As the white dries and soaks into the fabric, it often becomes less opaque. These whites can be tinted to make pastels and will print successfully on white or light color fabric.

The Gocco White ink made for the Stamp Kit For Cloth is more opaque than many white inks, but it will not completely cover a dark color.

HEAT SETTING

Water-based textile inks must be heat set before laundering. The easiest way to heat set is with an iron. Home clothes dryers do not get hot enough, but commercial dryers are hotter and may work. Read the instructions that come with the ink and test first!

A few water-based inks are cured by adding a catalyst to the ink. These do not need to be heat set which saves time when doing a lot of printing. Mix catalyst only with the amount of ink that will be used within a day or two.

PUFF PAINT

Puff paint is a special kind of water-based ink. Some are white, but can be tinted; others are colored. Heat applied to the printed ink causes the ink to puff up. A heat gun works well, but a hair dryer may not be hot enough. If you use an iron, hold the iron above, not on, the ink.

SQUEEGEE HINTS

SIZE OF SQUEEGEE

The squeegee must be at least a little wider than the design, so the squeegee will extend across the width of the design. Printing a wide design with two or more passes of a narrow squeegee can leave ridges of ink on the printed surface. On the other hand, the squeegee should be narrower than the inside width of the frame so there is room to pull the squeegee over the screen. These considerations are in the plan-ahead-category that we sometime forget about in the heat of creativity.

TYPES OF SQUEEGEES

Light weight squeegees, included in the Screen Kit PG, are fine, but if you are going to be doing much printing you may like the heft of a larger squeegee with a wooden handle. Screen supply stores sell squeegees by the inch, so you can have one cut to the exact size you want.

HOLDING THE SQUEEGEE

POSITION

Hold the squeegee at a 45° angle to the screen. The squeegee will not push enough ink through the screen if the squeegee is held in a more upright manner, closer to perpendicular to the screen. On the other hand, if the squeegee is held too flat to the screen, it will squeeze ink under the screen and print a smudged image. Look carefully at the squeegee angle before you start printing. You want to maintain the 45° angle for the entire length of the screen. Practice this a few times.

Position the Master so you pull the squeegee from top to bottom towards you. This is much easier that pulling crosswise.

Correct 45° angle to hold squeegee

PRESSURE
Use even, moderate pressure and speed for the entire length of the stroke. Too much pressure can cause a rash of pin dots by forcing ink through tiny holes in the Master. Too little pressure will not push enough ink through the Master. Experiment a bit to get the feel. A few practice strokes will help you print smoothly.

PRINTING

PREPARATION
Have all supplies at hand: squeegee, ink, spatula to scoop ink out of container, paper and fabric for test prints, paper toweling or rags.

Have fabric ready to print, attached to an adhesive board, and with guide marks, if needed. (See STAMP KIT FOR CLOTH, PRINTING SURFACE: ADHESIVE BOARDS, p. 158.)

NEATNESS
Neatness counts...a lot! You do not want to ruin a shirt with a smudge of ink! Even though textile ink requires heat setting to be washable, it is almost impossible to remove smudges completely even though not yet heat set.

- Try to keep extra ink confined to the reservoir areas of screen.

- Do not let ink get on frame of Screen Master or squeegee handle. From there to fingers to shirt is an easy trip!
- Be careful not to get any ink on the bottom of screen or frame. It's easy to do, and you don't see the ink until it appears on your garment! Set inked Screen down carefully on a clean surface, and don't pick it up with inky fingers.

TEST PRINTS

APPLYING INK

- Apply ink either along the reservoir area at one end of PG Master for the width of the design plus a bit more.

Ink reservoir on PG 702 Master

Ink reservoirs on PG 701 Masters

- Sometime it is easier to scoop ink out of the jar with a tongue depressor or palette knife and put it directly on the squeegee. Be careful that a glob of ink does not drop onto your project!

- Use enough ink to print the entire length of the design. As you pull the squeegee down the screen, you need to maintain a bead of ink along the squeegee blade. Large, solid designs will need much more ink than line drawings. If the bead of ink runs out, that area will not print. Add more ink and pull the squeegee over the entire design again. Use a "generous amount" of ink. (Experience will tell you just how much this is.)

PIN DOTS

Do a test print first to get the feel of the squeegee and to check for pin dots. You may be dismayed that your first print is covered with tiny pin dots.

- Excessive pressure on the squeegee can cause a rash of pin dots. Be sure to use only enough pressure to get an even solid print.

- Wait a minute and make another print. Ink dries quickly in these tiny holes and clogs them. Many of the smallest pin dots will have disappeared.

- To eliminate the remaining pin dots, scrape excess ink off the Master, and turn Master shiny side up.

- Use the last test sheet as a guide to location of pin dots. The dots will show up on the shiny surface of Screen Master as dull specks.

- Paint Correction Fluid over these dots. Stay away from the image. Wait a few seconds for fluid to dry.

- Try another test print. Are all the pin dots gone? Repeat if you missed any.

- Note: Mimeo correction fluid available at office supply stores or nail polish also work as substitutes for Correction Fluid.

PRINT AWAY!

Make a trial print or two on the same kind of fabric as your project fabric. Once everything is fine, print away! Have everything ready so you can print easily and quickly.

CLOGGED SCREEN

Try not to stop in the middle of a run so ink does not dry in the screen and clog it. On long runs or on dry days ink will be more apt to happen. Fine lines will be the first areas to become clogged, so watch them carefully as you print. Here are some solutions:

- Turn the screen over, shiny side up and wipe over the image area with a wet cloth to dissolve the dried ink. Wipe again with a dry cloth. Do a test print.

- Most lines of ink have a retarder to mix with the ink. Follow the manufacturers' instructions. Some white ink, for example, is so heavily pigmented that without a retarder it can quickly clog the screen, permanently.

- If you do have to stop for s short time, you can keep the screen from clogging by flooding the screen:
  - ♦ Use the squeegee to pull a thick coating of ink over the screen…like cake frosting!
  - ♦ When you resume printing, draw the squeegee over the screen as usual, pulling the ink as you go along.

COLOR EFFECTS

PRINTING A BLEND

This is an easy way get more than one color when printing with a squeegee.

- Mix a blend of colors that are adjacent on the color wheel: yellow, orange, red; green, blue, purple. Blends of complementary colors, e.g., red, green, do not work well, because the mix of complements is a brown-gray.

- Mix a tinted range: pink to red; gray to black.

- Place the blended colors either on the squeegee or on the Master. The squeegee will carry the bands of colors across the design. Each print will be a bit different. After 15 or 20 prints clean off the screen and squeegee and start over with fresh colors.

PRINTING COLOR ON COLOR

Fabric color will affect the color of the printed ink. Ink colors will be true when printed on white or light color fabric, but will change when printed on bright or dark colors.

Beware! Commercially printed shirts with bright colors printed on bright or dark fabrics are more than they appear to be: under the bright ink colors is a base printing of white. The white and color printing is done with two separate screens. This is a commercial process requiring special equipment.

With care and patience you can try printing both white and color with just one screen. It is easier to do with a bold design rather than very fine lines.

- Stabilize fabric by attaching it to a tacky base. (See STAMP KIT FOR CLOTH, ADHESIVE BOARDS, p. 178.)

- Position PG Master on fabric. Place 2" long strips of masking tape on fabric along both sides of all four corners of Master to make corner marks. (Masking tape makes a more precise line than fabric marking pens make.)

- Hold Master firmly along tape marks. Another pair of hands is helpful. Print white ink. Remove Master.

- Clean Master.

- Let white ink dry. If you are impatient, use a hair dryer.

- Reposition Master *exactly* along tape marks. You will see the white image through the Master. Print the color.

- Does a trace of white show around some of the color? Paint over it with a fine brush using some of the color ink diluted with a little water so if flows better.

USING PRINT MASTERS

Did you know? You can also use an exposed Print Master to print with a squeegee, but why would you want to print with a squeegee when it is so simple to put the Print Master in the Printer and print away?

Printing with a squeegee allows you to use a wide array of screen printing inks that print very well with Print Masters and a squeegee, but are too thin to use in the Printer. Used in the Printer they will produce a smudgy image, but used with a squeegee will print a crisp image.

It is convenient to remove the Mylar top sheet from the Print Master. The sheet will only get in the way when printing with a squeegee. Then treat the Print Master as a PG Master.

REGISTRATION

Registration with PG Masters is very the same as registration with the Stamp Kit For Cloth. Review STAMP KIT FOR CLOTH, REGISTRATION, p. 159.

HINGE FOR SCREEN MASTER

Another way to register items is to hinge one side of the framed Screen Master to a work surface. Hinging the frame to a stationary surface secures frame so image always prints in the same place.

MAKING A HINGE

It is easy to make a temporary hinge with masking, strapping or duct tape. Type of tape depends on frame size and the number of prints needed. To hinge the light weight PG Masters, for instance, masking tape is fine.

- Place frame on table with shiny side of Screen Master facing table.
- Cut a strip of tape at least 1″ wide and the length of frame.

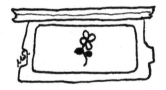

PG Master with tape hinge

- Place tape along the far back edge of frame so half the width of the tape runs along edge of frame and the other half is on the table. Fold tape in half lengthwise with fold in the juncture of frame and table. Press tape down securely.
- Hinge allows you to lift up frame by its front edge just as you lift the Gocco Printer.

- For extra stability, lift up frame and run another strip of tape along inside of hinge. Again place tape so half is on frame and half is on table.

PRINTING WITH HINGED MASTER

- Tape a piece of paper to table where image will print. Make first print on paper. Let ink dry. This is a guide to show where image will print.

Hinged PG Master with guide paper on table

- Place item to be printed over guide paper. Adjust placement and mark position. (See REGISTRATION, PRECISE PAPER PLACEMENT, p. 119.)

LIMITATIONS OF PRINTING WITH HINGED MASTER

- This method does not work well printing on thick, bulky items, e.g., sweat shirts.
- It works best on paper, ribbon or other flat items with hard edges that can be used for exact registration.

CLEAN UP

Pull squeegee over the Master to remove extra ink. Wipe remaining ink off PG Master with damp toweling. Do not wash PG Masters. The cardboard frame does not take to water.

PG Kit instructions recommend cleaning ink only off the image area and leaving ink to dry on the rest of the Master to keep any pin dots plugged. This is all right unless next time you use a different color ink. The new ink may soften the residue of old ink and mix with it. It is better to clean Master completely.

Promptly wash squeegee and clean up so ink doesn't dry on your tools.

STORAGE

Dry the PG Master with toweling and store it in a flat place, between two pieces of cardboard to protect it and avoid warping.

REUSE PG MASTERS

The Screen Master in PG Masters is more durable than the PG cardboard frame. After repeated printing and cleaning, the frame looses its firmness and will not hold the screen taut and flat, so it will not print clear, crisp images.

Save the screen by pulling it from the cardboard frame and remounting it on a more rigid frame. Use stretcher bars, available at art and craft stores. Attach Screen Master to frame with heavy duty double stick tape.

CARE OF PRINTED ITEMS

HEAT SETTING

Water-based textile inks need to be heat set to make them washable (unless a catalyst is added to the ink). Allow ink to dry completely. Cover the image with a pressing cloth or paper. Generally, ironing for two minutes is recommended. Be sure to iron the *entire* design! For large quantities, a commercial dryer may be hot enough to set the ink. A T-shirt transfer press works well. Be sure to read the instructions included with your ink for specific information, and always do some tests first.

LAUNDERING

Follow the instructions with the specific ink you are using. Many inks benefit from a seven day curing time after heat setting before laundering.

Ink colors will stay bright if washed with warm water and no bleach. Pearlescent and luminescent inks retain their luster if laundered carefully: gentle cycle, mild soap, garment turned inside out.

POSSIBILITIES

Here are a few projects to try, other surfaces to embellish.

PAPER

You can use Gocco High Mesh Ink, the ink that came with your Printer, for printing on paper with PG Masters. Water-based inks such as textile ink may not be suitable for printing on paper, since their high water content can make paper buckle. High Mesh ink, with a lower water content, is perfect, and can be used with a squeegee even though we usually think of it as just "Print Master Ink." Clean up with Goop, the same as cleaning a Print Master.

- Print on items too large to fit in either printer: shopping bags, paper table cloths, paper aprons and bibs, etc.
- Print designs larger than the image area of a Print Master, e.g., posters, flyers, broadsides.

ENAMEL INK

Enamel screen printing ink is an oil-based ink, used for printing on slick, shiny, nonporous surfaces: metal, Mylar, glass, Lucite, even slick paper. You may have tried printing on these surfaces with the Printer and found that ink coverage is fair. Enamel ink will give an opaque, shiny coating. Enamel ink is slow drying. Allow about 12 hours before stacking printed items.

A FEW IDEAS

Mirror Card is a very shiny card stock with a mirror-bright finish. Enamel ink on mirror card is striking! Other ideas for enamel ink are metal trophy plaques, mirrors, notebooks and ring binders, Lucite, wood objects, ceramic tile, Mylar balloons.

CLEAN UP

Clean with mineral spirits or turpentine, use rubber gloves and have good ventilation.

GLASS ETCHING

Etching cream is water-based and may be screen printed on glass.

- Clean glass thoroughly. Be careful not to leave fingerprints on glass. Oily finger prints will repel etching compound.
- Wear rubber gloves to protect skin.

ETCHING FLAT SURFACES
Flat surfaces such as mirrors and windows are two good surfaces to start on.

- Using a squeegee, screen print etching compound on glass.
- Lift up screen, leave etching compound on glass for about ten minutes, wash off. (The compound stops working after about ten minutes.)

ETCHING CURVED SURFACES
Glassware is the most common curved surface to etch.

- Remove PG Master from cardboard frame. Tape Master securely and tightly to glass. Carefully dab etching compound evenly on image area of Master. Be careful not to get etching compound on other areas of the glass.
- Leave Master in place until it is time to rinse etching compound off glass, otherwise etching compound may smear.

POTTERY AND CERAMICS
Print flat pieces of unglazed or glazed pottery using a squeegee and PG Master.

Print designs on special decal paper and then transfer the design to pottery. This is a good method to use on curved or uneven surfaces.

PRINTED CIRCUIT BOARDS
The technically minded can make a Screen Master of a computer circuit pattern for a circuit board. There are many computer programs that can produce circuit designs. Those of you who specialize in printed circuit boards will know how the details work. This is the essence of the process:

- Print circuit design on circuit board with an acid resist ink.

- After ink dries, immerse printed board in an acid bath that will eat away area of the board not covered by ink.
- Wash ink off with a special solvent. The printed circuit remains on the board.

PROJECTS

A FEW WORDS ON CREATIVITY

WHO NEEDS A PRINT GOCCO?

IDEAS AND INSPIRATIONS

PROJECTS

A FEW WORDS ON CREATIVITY
The Gocco printers are a spring board to creativity. This is the fun part!

POSSIBILITIES
Many chapters of this manual conclude with a POSSIBILITIES section that presents ideas and uses for that particular aspect of Gocco printing, e.g., the FELT PRINTING CHAPTER, p. 107 ends with ideas for using the Felt Sheets.

The information in this chapter is more general. This is just a beginning. The excitement will be in your own applications. Lest the mere thought of coming up with new ideas for your Gocco Printer, or being creative, puts you in a cold sweat, relax for a moment and read on:

WE ALL HAVE IT!
Do not assume that creativity is something you either have or do not have, period. Consider the ability to "be creative" a skill that one can develop and strengthen. This is not unlike learning to play the piano or studying a foreign language. It's hard work and unfamiliar territory at first, then it becomes a way of thinking.

TOTAL IMMERSION
New ideas flourish in an environment of total immersion. The more you look around you for ideas, the more you will see. The seeds of potential projects are in the graphics of magazine ads, the catalogs bulging in your mail box, wrapping paper, greeting cards, posters, books of quotations.

Keep your scissors handy. Clip out things that catch your eye. Think of your clipping file as a repository for latent ideas. Browse through it occasionally. One image can trigger a chain reaction of inspirations. Most commercial designs are copyright protected. Use them as a spring board to encourage your own ideas. Example: The color scheme of orange, red and magenta for a Valentine card came from a box of decongestant tablets.

GERMINATION

The easy side of developing creativity is to spend some time being passive, daydreaming, letting your thoughts wander. This idle-appearing activity is an important complement to time spent actively looking, searching, for ideas. The brain thrives in the slack time. This is when ideas germinate.

Performing mundane activities helps the mind to wander, e.g., showering, vacuuming. These activities require just enough concentration to block out distractions while allowing the mind to meander. These are often the times when you will get your best inspirations. Keep notebooks at hand to jot or sketch ideas so they are not forgotten and lost. (For more practical information on developing creativity read THE CREATIVE SPIRIT, see APPENDIX, BIBLIOGRAPHY, p. 235.)

WHO NEEDS A PRINT GOCCO?

Projects and Gocco printing are synonymous. The Gocco printer is an invaluable tool for crafters, schools, clubs, small businesses, ad infinitum.

ARTISTS

The Printer is a creative and expressive tool for many artists' ideas.

- Calligraphy
- Commission work
- Custom invitations and stationery
- Graphic art comps
- Greeting cards
- Handmade printed books
- Limited edition prints
- Wearable art

ATHLETIC TEAMS

Teams, from children's to adult's, can use the Gocco to identify their team and to recognize outstanding effort.

- Awards, ribbons buttons, certificates

- Fund raising
- Pennants
- Publicity flyers, event schedules, postcards
- Uniforms: Shirts, jackets, shorts, caps, even socks!

BUSINESSES

The Gocco can save money in printing costs, quickly producing custom items for a fraction of the cost of commercial printing. It has a multitude of uses for small and medium size businesses.

- Appointment cards
- Catalogs
- Coupons
- Displays
- Emblems
- Flyers: announcements, banners, brochures, promotions, sales
- Forms
- Gift certificates
- Hang tags for clothing
- Letterhead stationery, envelopes, business cards
- Newsletters
- Notebooks
- Price lists
- Proposals
- Questionnaires

- Reminder notices and post cards
- Shopping bags and boxes
- Signs
- Uniforms: shirts, aprons, jackets, caps, scarves

CLUBS AND ORGANIZATIONS

Youth groups, civic clubs and charities will find the Printers an asset.

FUND RAISING

- Greeting cards
- Personalized custom-printed stationery
- Raffle and admission tickets
- Recipe collections
- T-shirts, aprons, tote bags, pennants

PUBLICITY

- Event notices, flyers, posters
- Postcards

RECOGNITION

- Awards, certificates, prize ribbons
- Badges, patches
- Uniforms

CRAFTS

Gocco printing and crafts are almost synonymous. Craft persons use the Gocco directly and indirectly in their work, both to make items and to label and advertise them.

- Bags and boxes
- Buttons, pins, earrings
- Calendars
- Earrings
- Florist ribbon
- Greeting cards
- Hang tags
- Balsa wood models

- Note pads
- Paper napkins
- Stationery
- Streamers
- Wrapping paper, tissue paper, and coordinated ribbon

RESTAURANTS AND CATERERS

- Aprons
- Doggie bags
- Food basket enclosures
- Gift certificates
- Menus, menu covers, menu inserts, daily specials
- Napkins
- Paper table cloths, place mats, and bibs
- Table notices

SCHOOLS

CHILDREN'S ART
Young children's art is most effective printed with a Gocco. Once set up, the Printers are so easy to use that even preschoolers can make their own prints. Print on school tablet paper or construction paper to complete the look.

ART PROJECTS
Art teachers of all grade levels can incorporate the Gocco into their curriculum in many ways:

- Book making
- Color theory projects
- Drawing
- Fabric printing
- Mixed media
- Printmaking
- Screen printing

GENERAL SCHOOL USES

- Awards, certificates, diplomas, ribbons
- Badges, name tags
- Calendars
- Exhibits
- Fund raising
- Gifts
- Lunch sacks
- Newsletters and mastheads
- Pennants
- Program covers
- Publishing newsletters and books
- Publicity, posters, notices
- School motto
- Stationery, greeting cards
- Yearbooks

THERAPISTS

Art therapists and rehabilitation professionals are well aware of the therapeutic value of art in our lives. The Print Gocco can be an important part of their work.

IDEAS AND INSPIRATIONS

GIFTS

It is so easy to print napkins, note paper, bags, even dish towels, that you can build a nice cache of unique, but inexpensive, gift items to present at a moment's notice for a last-minute gift. Having your creations stashed away for gifts is like money in the bank!

NAPKINS

Printing paper napkins is an excellent first project for the owner of a new Gocco. Personalized napkins have many uses:

- Hostess gifts
- Home, boats, summer cabins
- Parties: birthdays, graduations, housewarmings, showers, weddings, bon voyage, etc. Print extra for the honored guest to keep.
- Print a napkin to use as a party invitation.

LUNCH BAGS

Printing lunch bags is another easy beginning project. In addition to brown bags, some supermarkets carry colored bags and wine bags. For large quantities, check local paper companies in the Yellow Pages.

- Bags are not just for lunch. Use them as "containers" for gifts.

- Print a Valentine or Halloween motif and fill bags with goodies
- For lunch-carriers, print *"BROWN BAG"* in brown ink on brown bags.

Brown bag

STATIONERY

Personalized stationery is very satisfying. With little effort you can have colorful stationery with pizzazz. On one master there is room for a flourished name and a return address for envelopes...nice for yourself and impressive for gifts.

GREETING CARDS

Making greeting cards is often the inspiration for purchasing a Gocco.

- Go through the calendar and you'll find excuses to send your creative cards for numerous occasions. This makes keeping in touch with family and friends easy.

- It is so easy to print a couple dozen colorful Valentines, that you can send love notes to *all* your Valentine sweet hearts!!!

- Print a mask/Halloween card.

- Save on postage and print post cards. They are quick and easy to do.

NEW BABY

- Print birth announcements on the smallest disposable diapers.
- For a baby girl print copies of her foot prints in pink ink with the caption, *"We are tickled pink!"*
- Welcome a new baby with personalized diapers. Who else will give such an unusual gift to the proud parents! Print some note cards with the baby's name; the parents can use them for thank you notes. Attach the Master to the hand-held Stamp Kit for Cloth and print baby's name on tissue paper, wrapping paper, wide florist ribbon, and even the mailing box.
- Don't stop yet, there's more! Clean the Master, reink with Cloth Ink and personalize some tiny shirts, bibs, crib sheets…What fun!

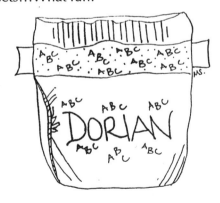

NEWSLETTERS

Family newsletters for holidays or just to keep in touch are easy and colorful. Print them on a separate sheet to include with a card, or even as a post card.

RECIPE CARDS

- Print personalized recipe cards for your self and for other cooks.
- Print copies of your favorite recipes to give as gifts.
- If you give food as a gift, include the recipe.
- Print your family's favorite recipes for a family reunion.

PARTIES

A great advantage of the Gocco is the ability to custom-coordinate all aspects of a party. Carry out themes and colors on many items not available in stationery stores.

- Banners: use adding machine tape for long paper "banners" or streamers
- Coasters, paper napkins, place mats, and table cloths
- Doggie bags
- Favors
- Invitations
- Menus
- Name tags
- Party hats
- Personalized toilet paper. Yes, it has been done!
- Place cards
- Ribbon streamers for tables or bouquets
- RSVP cards

- Table decorations
- Thank you notes
- Tooth pick "flags"

    Print several flags on one Master. Cut them apart and
    glue two flags, back-to-back sandwiching in a tooth
    pick or skewer.

THE PRINTER AS ENTERTAINMENT:

- Have the guests sign in using the Gocco fine-
  pointed pen. Use the sign in sheet to make a Master
  and let everyone print their autographs on napkins
  or lunch bags.

- For a child's birthday, prepare a few Masters to print lunch bags. Each child can go home with an assortment of colorful bags.

- Prior to a holiday, e.g., Valentine's Day, have a card printing party. Guests can design and print cards, envelopes, post cards, all ready to mail. Guests can bring colored papers, glitter, embossing powders and other add-ons to vary designs. (See MIXED MEDIA CHAPTER, p. 81.)

- Print a joke or riddle in the middle of an 8$\frac{1}{2}$" x 11" piece of card stock. Cut paper in quarters making four post cards. Mail one a day. Your recipient will have to wait four days to piece together the story!

BIRTHDAYS...PLAN AHEAD

Print all your birthday cards in January. Make this one of your New Year's resolutions. Do one design for the year and everyone on your list gets that card. Next year do a new design. Who knows, these could become collector's items.

You could even address and stamp your cards, ready for mailing throughout the year. (Impress your friends!) All you have to do is remember to mail them on time!

BUTTONS

With a BADGE A MINIT button maker, it is easy to make personalized button pins. (See APPENDIX, OTHER SUPPLIES)

BLANK PUZZLES

Blank puzzles can be a palette for witty cards. Mail the puzzles in pieces; the recipient can "put it all together!"

Blank puzzles are available at many rubber stamp and card stores. Mail these puzzles minus one piece:

 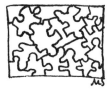

- Don't miss the "peace" of Christmas.
- You have a piece of my heart
- Something's missing without you!

Note: Ink builds up on the Master where the cracks are on the puzzle. This deposit of ink will transfer to the next puzzle unless a print is made on scrap paper after printing each puzzle.

LABELS

Make personalized labels and stickers. Blank pressure sensitive labels come in many sizes and colors. (Avery is a common brand.) Cut sheets of dry gum (lick and stick) paper to size and use for labels. Dry gum paper comes in glossy finish such as Krome Kote or in matte finish. Printing on matte-finish paper dries faster than printing on glossy or pressure sensitive paper.

- Book plates
- Bumper stickers
- Children's belongings
- Container labels
- Custom/decorative stickers
- Gourmet food: jams, pickles, vinegar, etc.
- Holiday stickers for packages and cards
- Luggage tags (may be laminated after printing.)
- Mailing labels
- Name tags
- Notebooks
- Return address labels

- Seals to coordinate with your
  Gocco-printed stationery

PENNANTS!

Cut triangular pennant shapes out of felt and print on them with the Gocco...just the same as paper. There is no need to use fabric ink; these are never going to be washed. Do a dozen, hang them side-by-side from a cord, and string up for party decorations.

- Clubs
- School
- Souvenirs
- Sports
- Yachting.

NEEDLEWORK

CROSS STITCH

Needlework? Save time and *print* a cross stitch pattern rather than stitching it. "Printed" cross stitch can almost pass for the real thing! There are even some computer fonts derived from cross-stitched letters.

DOLLS

Doll makers can use the Gocco to print faces on cloth dolls rather than stitching them, or print a pattern in a light color and stitch over it.

DIFFERENT SURFACES

There seems to be no end to the ingenious uses for the Print Gocco:

- Balloons: blow up half way, print, and then finish inflating. (Printing vanishes if done on an uninflated balloon which is later inflated.

- Black velvet!

- Easter eggs: use the Stamper and roll-print the Master over the curved surface. Print smooth rocks the same way.

- Feathers

- Leather, Ultra Suede

- Leaves…print on flattened dried fall leaves.

See how creative you can be!

TROUBLESHOOTING

PLAN AHEAD

PREPARING ORIGINAL

BULB PROBLEMS

INSPECT EXPOSED MASTER

EXPOSING LARGE SOLID AREAS

FILTER PROBLEMS

"WINDOW" PROBLEMS

INK PROBLEMS

TACKY BASE LOSES TACKINESS

TROUBLESHOOTING

Gocco printing is fun and easy; a way to express ideas and creativity. A Gocco will print on just about anything that will stay still for a minute. It will do much more than first meets the eye, but, alas, a Gocco Printer is not flawless. This section is about the frustrations encountered when things are less than perfect.

The most important part of troubleshooting is prevention, to forestall problems before the hair-pulling stage. The second part is to diagnose and remedy the problem. Once is bad enough, but repeatedly having the same problem is maddening.

PLAN AHEAD

Build some leeway into your schedule. Remember Murphy's law: if there are going to be problems, they will happen at the last minute, on the last Master, immediately before an important project has to be finished.

Have extra supplies on hand, just in case. Masters and bulbs are like chocolate chip cookies. You don't want to be down to the last one! Plan your colors, check your ink supply.

For a project requiring envelopes, select envelopes first. The available sizes and colors of envelopes is more limited than the choice of papers.

PREPARING THE ORIGINAL

Care in preparation of the original design is the single most important part of successful printing. Review PREPARING DESIGNS, p. 29, for many hints not mentioned here.

PHOTO COPIES

Photo copy machines have become indispensable to modern life...imagine not having access to one! They are also invaluable to fans of the Gocco Printers. Convert any non-carbon artwork to a carbon original via the toner of a copy machine. BUT, there is "no free lunch!"

Photo copies are also the single largest source of frustration when exposing a Master. Copy machine toner is more concentrated than the carbon in pens or inks. Using a

Blue Filter when exposing a Master minimizes, but does not eliminate, problems caused by toner. Prevention is by far the best cure when working with photo copies.

PHOTO COPY GUIDES

- Set copy machine on the light side of medium. Make several copies at different settings, marking the copies for reference. It is most frustrating to get home and then need one more copy; far better to spend a little extra for copies, saving time and energy for your projects.

- Avoid, like the plague, photo copies that have specks, dots, or gray smudges of toner. Set the copy machine lighter or use a different copier. Your eye may ignore these specks, but the Gocco will pick them up.

- A copy machine may make perfect copies of line art, but on large black areas the toner may have a slight sheen. Shiny surfaces reflect heat from the flash bulbs, so the Master will not expose completely even though there is plenty of carbon in the toner. After flashing, the sheen often disappears, so it's hard to determine if the toner was shiny. Setting the copy machine lighter generally does not help. Try another copier.

- As a very last resort to remedy a photo copy that is too dark, try dusting the copy with powdered white Conté Crayon or white chalk.
    - Rub the chalk on fine sandpaper.
    - Sprinkle this dust over photo copy, and gently wipe off with paper toweling leaving a fine dusting on paper.
    - Expose as usual with Filter.
    - This method is only marginally successful, but in an emergency it may help.

- Beware of your favorite copier. Copy machines need regular servicing, but some stores neglect this. A machine that made perfect copies 5,000 copies ago may not to do so now.

- There is no way to measure the amount of carbon/toner in a photo copy to know if the toner is just right…frustrating. We have only the guidelines just listed, and our right brain hunches.

- Always use the Blue Filter when exposing a Master from a photo copy. The Filter is placed between the Printer "window" and the Master. Remember, "Filter first."

- Using two Filters does not help expose the Master if the photo copy is very dark.

- Use the Filter *only* for photo copies. If you have a design that is a combination of photo copies and drawn or other non-photo copy elements, photo copy the entire piece.
    - ♦ Sometime it is possible to slide the Filter off to the side. Part of the Filter will extend outside the Printer to the left or right, so the Filter covers only the photo copied area of a design.
    - ♦ Parts of an old Filter may be cut apart. Use a piece of Filter to cover just the photo copied area of the design.

BULB PROBLEMS

BULBS FAILED TO FLASH

- The Gocco Flash Bulbs are very reliable, only rarely does one fail to flash. If a bulb fails, replace *all* bulbs and expose Master again. Not enough heat is generated to expose Master properly if just one bulb is replaced. It is the *combined* heat of all the bulbs that exposes the Master.

- Check the batteries. The batteries last a long time, but not forever.

- Check contacts:
    - ♦ The silvery strips on the flash housing should touch the contacts on the printer. Gently pull them out a bit them if they are not touching.
    - ♦ Open the battery compartment and make sure the batteries are held snugly in place.

OTHER BULBS

Did you use Gocco bulbs? Camera flash bulbs, a vanishing species, will flash, but do produce enough heat to expose the Master as well as the Gocco bulbs. Flash bulbs are made to produce light; Gocco bulbs are made to produce heat. In the Gocco process, light is incidental. (In a dire emergency, try camera flash bulbs and a darker photo copy.)

INSPECT EXPOSED MASTER

Avoid frustration before inking and printing. Inspect your exposed Master carefully. It is frustrating to ink an exposed Master and start printing only to realize that the Master is not printing well. Develop the habit of looking before inking. But what are you looking for?

WHAT TO LOOK FOR

MASTER WELL EXPOSED

- Look first at an unexposed Master and note how the printing side, the blue side, is evenly shiny.

- Exposed areas of a Master are dull where the shiny saran film has melted away. Well exposed areas should be evenly dull without shiny spots.

- After exposing, original design will adhere to Master. Inking the Master is easier if the original design is still adhering to the Master. You can pull up edges of original enough to see if there are any problems. You can also entirely remove the original for closer inspection, then reposition it, securing original lightly to Master with small bits of masking tape for inking.

- Perhaps the original has *not* adhered to the Master after exposing: bulbs flashed, lift up top of printer, and there's your original, still on the foam base! After exposing a Master, the original should adhere to Master. If the design has not adhered to the Master, Master probably has not been exposed completely. You will see little or no evidence of your design on the Master.
  - ◆ Original was not a carbon black. There probably was not enough carbon in the

design. Remember that many pens that look very black contain dye-based ink, not carbon.

♦ Original was glossy or semi-glossy.
♦ One or more bulbs failed to flash.
♦ Look carefully at the Master. It probably shows little or no trace of the design melted in to the shiny saran film. If the Master is still perfectly even and shiny, it is all right to expose it again. Discard Master if there is even just a faint hint of the image melted in to the saran film

PIN DOTS

Pin dots appear as tiny dull specks. Tilting the exposed side of the Master under bright light will make it easier to detect them. A few are not a problem, but "rashes" can be impossible to eliminate.

- Minute specks of toner are sometime scattered over a photo copy. These become flagrantly obvious when printing. Using a Blue Filter minimizes pin dots, but will not always eliminate them.

- Paint over pin dots with Gocco Correction Fluid on the outside of Master, (the shiny saran film). This will plug up the pin dots so ink cannot go through them when printing. You can also use White Out, Liquid Paper, or nail polish. Allow a minute drying time. You can do this before inking Master or when printing if you see more pin dots. Use the Gocco print as a guide.

- Large areas of pin dots not close to the design can be covered with strips of tape placed on Master.

- It may be easier to expose another Master than to try fixing large areas of pin dots that are interspersed throughout a design.

TONER ADHERING TO THE MASTER

When you remove the photo copy from the exposed Master, there may be a heavy coating of black toner adhering to the Master and very little toner left on the photo copy paper. The Master is exposed, but will not print well because toner is plugging the holes in the Master.

- Turpentine, charcoal lighter, or cigarette lighter (*not* paint thinner!) will come to your rescue. Pour a bit on the blue side of the Master and gently rub the toner off with paper toweling. Don't scrub off every speck of black, or you will damage the Master. A gray residue is O.K. Note: There are other solvents such as automobile carburetor cleaner that will remove the carbon, but they will also dissolve the Master!

- This will solve your immediate problem, but in the future, save your self this hassle and set the copy machine lighter or use a different copier. Some types of toner, especially from Kodak copiers, adhere to the Master. This also happens if the copy machine is set too dark.

- Did you use the blue filter? Always use the Filter with photo copies. The Filter will minimize this problem, but will not eliminate it if the copy is very dark.

EXPOSING SEVERAL MASTERS

If you are working on a complex project requiring more than one Master, you will probably prepare all your art work first, expose all the Masters, then... Stop! Expose *one* Master. Inspect it carefully to be sure it is properly exposed. If all is fine, *then* expose the next Master.

NOT SURE?

If you are uncertain that a Master is properly exposed, ink just a portion of it, and print that part to see how it looks. This will help you know what to look for next time. With an observant, critical eye you can learn much.

EXPOSING LARGE SOLID AREAS

Large solid areas are the one less-than-perfect aspect of Gocco printing. Printing large solid areas can be difficult and frustrating. After flashing, there may be small, shiny, unexposed spots, like reverse freckles.

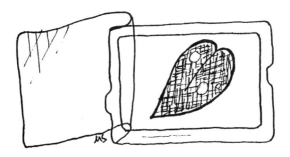

Exposed Master showing unexposed spots

CURE

- Scratch gently at the unexposed spots with a fine needle until the shiny area is scratched away. Be careful not to scratch so much that you wear a hole in the Master.

- Another solution is to expose the Master again. Yes, that means more bulbs.
    - ◆ Remove original from Master.
    - ◆ Directly on the outside of the Master, color over the unexposed areas with a Gocco or other carbon pen.

Master with unexposed sots colored over with a carbon pen

- ◆ Put Master back in printer. Place a piece of plain white paper on foam base. Do not use original.
- ◆ Flash. The carbon pen that you used to "color in" the unexposed dots will absorb heat from the bulbs and melt away the unexposed areas.

PREVENTION

SCREENING
Screening changes a solid area into a dotted one. A "screen" is a clear Mylar sheet covered with tiny white dots. Use the Photo Screen for Gocco Printers, see PHOTO SCREEN CHAPTER, p. 99. Screens of different line and texture densities are also available at some graphic art stores.

- Place screen on copy machine. Lay your design face down on screen and photo copy.
- Your photo copy will be dotted rather than solid. These dotted areas expose better than solid ones.

Screened solid areas

- Put several sheets of plain white paper on Foam Base of Printer before exposing Master. This will press original closer to Master and ensure better exposure.
- Use Blue Filter and expose Master.
- The resulting Gocco print will look almost solid, as the tiny dots nearly merge together when printed.

CROSS HATCH
Redraw the solid area with cross hatching or another rough texture.

Cross hatch patterns

THE GOCCO PENS

Even though these pens contain carbon, they can cause problems. The ink needs to be very dry before it will expose the Master. The outline will dry first and expose well, but the filled-in area will expose irregularly. Dry to the touch is not enough. When filling in a large solid area, hasten the drying with a hair dryer or allow a few hours to air dry.

FILTER PROBLEMS

RUINED FILTER

Remember, "Filter first." Perhaps you forgot that the Filter is next to the Printer "Window," sandwiched between the Window and the Master. It is easy to reverse the order, putting the Filter in the Printer last, so the Filter is touching the photo copy when the Master is exposed. Toner from the photo copy will fuse to the Filter.

If you forget and ruin your Filter, there is still hope. The carbon residue on the Filter will expose on the next Master, but you can cut your Filter apart and salvage the good parts. These odd pieces may be useful when exposing an original which is only part photo copy. You may be able to slide a piece of Filter in between Master and window to cover just the photo copied area.

OLDER PRINTERS

You will also ruin the Filter if you put in just the Filter and forget to put in the Master. This is possible with the older orange and yellow B6 Printers that don't have the safeguard button to prevent flashing the bulbs when a Master is not in place.

FILTER WITH "REAL" ORIGINALS

Use the Filter only with photo copies. Did you forget and use the filter with a "real" original? The Master will not expose completely, producing a print that has a sandy, irregular texture. Perhaps sometime you might want this effect. Now you know a way to achieve it!

"WINDOW" PROBLEMS

CLEANLINESS

The "Window" of the Printer is correctly called a stage glass, not very clear; but everyone can imagine a window. Take care to keep it clean. Put a piece of white paper in Printer. Lower Printer on paper and look through Window to see if Window is clean. Paint spots on Window can prevent Master from exposing. Clean with Master Cleaner, Goop or paint thinner.

OLDER PRINTERS

Because older orange and yellow B6 Printers that don't have the safeguard button to prevent flashing the bulbs when a Master is not in place, you can easily ruin the Window. Forget both Master and Filter and the photo copy toner will fuse to the plastic Window. This means you replace the Window! (This is not a problem with the B5 Printer which has a glass window.)

INK PROBLEMS

UNEVEN INKING

High Mesh Ink is too thick to spread out evenly on the Master when printing. Varying thickness of ink can cause ink to print unevenly. This is more evident when printing large solid areas than line drawings.

- After inking Master, use a spatula or stiff paper to smooth ink to an even thickness. When reinking a Master, lifting up the Mylar top sheet pulls the ink up in little mountains. Smooth out ink before replacing the Mylar sheet.

- For the B6 Printer make a cushion sheet out of a sheet of Ink Block or similar foam. This is helpful when printing a large solid area.
    - ◆ Leave Ink Block attached to its backing sheet so the Ink Block will not stick to either the Master or the Window of the Printer. Cut the sheet to $4^1/_4$" x $6^1/_8$", the size of the inside dimension of the B6 Master.
    - ◆ Place the cushion between the Master and the Printer Window, when placing the inked

Master in the Printer. The cushion will help to push the ink through the Master more evenly.

- The B5 Printer comes with a cushion sheet. The larger printing area of the B5 makes using a cushion sheet more important.

INK TEMPERATURE

- Ink temperature also affects printing quality. On hot days, ink is thinner, and more ink will pass through Master. This can produce a stippled, textured finish to the ink.
    - ♦ Refrigerating tubes of ink or the inked Master will thicken ink. (Note: Some inks, especially fluorescent inks are thinner than other colors.)
    - ♦ Refrigerate inked Master for 15 minutes. These are both temporary fixes, but they do work.

INK DRIES IN MASTER

HIGH MESH INK
Ink will dry in an inked Master if left exposed to the air for an hour our more

- First try printing several copies on scrap paper.

- Wiping the Master with paper toweling moistened with turpentine or mineral spirits is a quick fix to soften dried ink.

- Also try spreading a layer of Master Cleaner or Goop over the printing side of the Master and leaving it for 10 to 15 minutes. (Note: The "printing side" of the Master is the outside surface of the Master, the side that prints on the paper.) Wipe off Cleaner with toweling and try printing.

- Master Cleaner and Goop leave a residue on the Master that will transfer to your paper and may cause embossing powder to stick to the paper.

IMAGE SMEARED
Ink may smear as printed paper pulls off Master. If you pull the printed paper from the Master, take care not to drag the paper over the Master. (See TACKY BASE LOOSES TACKINESS, p. 228.)

INK FOR CLOTH

Be careful not to let this ink dry in the Master. This is a water-based ink and will dry much more quickly than High Mesh Ink which is an oil-water emulsion. If the Master is left exposed to the air for just 5 or 10 minutes, the ink will begin to dry.

- Wiping the outside of the Master with wet toweling should soften the ink. Stamp a couple times on scrap paper.
- If the ink has thoroughly dried for a longer time, it is impossible to soften it. Discard Master and start over.

PAPER RELATED PROBLEMS

- Slick or coated papers will show more ink unevenness than soft or absorbent papers. This, too, will be more apparent when printing large solid areas.
- Rough or textured paper will cause ink to print irregularly. When printing on rough paper, bumps of ink build up on the Master. These bumps will transfer to the next print leaving small globs of ink on the paper. Remedy this by printing one or two throw sheets on scrap paper after each print on rough paper.
- Some papers are not receptive to ink. Papers that are recommended for commercial printing have an ink receptive surface that will also work with Gocco printing.
- Ink may bleed on paper that is very absorbent, however we have printed successfully on paper toweling!
- Paper with inclusions, bits of petals or leaves for instance, can come loose and stick to the Master, clogging it. This can be a hassle.
- Note: See PAPER, p. 41.

TACKY BASE LOOSES TACKINESS

The purpose of the gray tack base is to hold paper in place when printing. After a while the base will pick up paper lint and loose it's tacky finish. The tackiness can be renewed in a couple ways:

- Press wide masking or scotch tape, sticky side down on to base. Repeat this a few times until tacky feel is restored.
- Remove Base from Printer and hold tacky pad under warm running water, being careful not to soak foam. Carefully run water over just the tacky surface, brushing surface with a soft brush. Shake off water. Let air dry. Don't dry with a towel.

In practice the tacky surface does not work well…it just is not sticky enough. If you want your paper to stay put, use double stick tape on the base to attack a paper securely to the base. Then rub Tack a Note repositionable glue stick on the paper. This will keep your printing paper in place, but allow you easily to remove the paper after printing.

Remember, look carefully, pay attention to detail, learn from your mistakes!

APPENDIX

BIBLIOGRAPHY

GOCCO PRINTERS AND SUPPLIES

OTHER SUPPLIES

GOCCO CARD COMPETITION

ABOUT THE AUTHOR

COLOPHON

APPENDIX

BIBLIOGRAPHY

Gocco printing goes hand-in-hand with paper crafts, bookmaking, and creativity, These publications and videos are a mother lode of stimulating ideas, sure to make your fingers pulsate and your Gocco Printer twitch!

BOOK MAKING

- BOOKCRAFT
    Anette Hollander
    Van Nostrand Reinhold Co., New York
    This is out of print; check your library.

- CREATIVE BOOKBINDING
    Pauline Johnson
    University of Washington Press, Seattle, WA

- NON-ADHESIVE BINDING
    Keith A. Smith
    The Sigma Foundation, Inc.
    155 S. Main St.
    Fairport, NY 14450

CLIP ART

There is much copyright-free art available. However, it is important to note that one can not "borrow" freely from just any source. Be sure that the image is indeed copyright-free, otherwise get written permission from the artist or find another source.

Dover has an extensive selection of copyright-free clip art books that are a wonderful aid to Gocco projects. These are only a few:

- AUTHENTIC ART DECO ALPHABETS

- CARTOUCHES AND DECORATIVE FRAMES

- DECORATIVE FRAMES AND BORDERS

- READY-TO-USE ARROWS

- READY-TO-USE BANNERS

- READY-TO-USE CHRISTMAS DESIGNS

- READY-TO-USE FOOD AND DRINK

- READY-TO-USE FLORAL DESIGNS
- READY-TO-USE HEADLINES
- NEW CALLIGRAPHIC ORNAMENTS & FLOURISHES by Arthur Baker
- TREASURY OF FLOWER DESIGNS by Susan Graber
  Dover Publications, Inc.
  31 East 2nd St.
  Mineola, NY 11501
- SCAN THIS BOOK
  John Mendenhall
  Published by Art Direction Book Company
  10 East 39th St.
  New York, NY 10016

Computer clip art is another vast resource to explore for Gocco images. Again, be sure that it is not copyright.

GOCCO REFERENCE BOOKS

- DESIGNING AND WORKING WITH GOCCO
  Shereen LaPlantz
  LaPlantz Studios
  P.O. Box 160
  Bayside, CA 95524
  $29.95, $4.50 s/h

This unique book contains seventeen wonderful Gocco printed examples showing the creative possibilities of Gocco printing along with the artist's helpful comments on each print. The prints include information on color charts, carbon blacks, photographs and printing papers. Honest and helpful information on what works and doesn't work.

- THE GOCCO Q & A HANDBOOK
  Joan B. Machinchick
  Lake Claire Design Studio
  1023 Lake Claire Dr.
  Annapolis, MD 21401
  $9.00

This is a quick reference book on commonly asked Gocco operating questions. The author writes from an extensive background of Gocco experience.

INSPIRATION

- THE CREATIVE SPIRIT
  Daniel Goleman, Paul Kaufman, Michael Ray
  Dutton, Published by the Penguin Group,
  1992
This is a wonderful presentation of the creative process
that can help spark our own creativity.

- ED EMBERLY'S DRAWING BOOK OF ANIMALS

- ED EMBERLY'S DRAWING BOOK OF FACES

- ED EMBERLY'S DRAWING BOOK, MAKE A WORLD

- ED EMBERLY'S GREAT THUMBPRINT DRAWING BOOK
  Little Brown and Co.
If you've ever said "I can't draw," these are the books for
you. No more excuses!

RUBBER STAMP PUBLICATIONS

These publications are a visual wonderland of ideas and
rubber stamps to incorporate into your Gocco printing.
Remember, rubber stamp images are copyrighted, and are
intended for personal, not commercial use. There are many
stamping newsletters and magazines. This is a one-stop
source for rubber stamp information.

- RUBBER STAMP SOURCEBOOK
  David Ward
  Cornucopia Press
  4739 University Way NE, Suite 1610-B
  Seattle, WA 98105

PAPER CRAFT BOOKS

- HOW TO MAKE POP-UPS
  Joan Irving
  Morrow Junior Books, New York

PAPER DREAMS
  Lorraine Bodger
  Universe Books, New York

- PAPER TRICKS
    Florence Temko
    Scholastic Inc., New York, Toronto, London,
        Auckland, Sydney

- UP-POPS-PAPER ENGINEERING WITH ELASTIC BANDS
    Mark Hiner
    Tarquin Publications
    Norfolk, 1P215JP, England

VIDEOS

These videos are an excellent supplement to a Gocco Printer. Add flair and creativity to your paper projects.

- CREATIVE CORRESPONDENCE
    Mary Worthington
    Fold notes, envelopes, cards, stationers folders.
        90 min. $25.00

- BAGS & BOXES
    Mary Worthington
    Instructions for several boxes, 7 bags, 60 min.
        $23.00
    Both videos are available:
    Think Ink
    7526 Olympic View Dr. Suite E
    Edmonds, WA 98026-5556

GOCCO PRINTERS AND SUPPLIES

PRINT GOCCO B6

SPECIFICATIONS

Dimensions 170mm (6 $3/4$") width x 150mm ($5^{15}/_{16}$") height x 380mm (15") length

Weight 1.3 kg, (2.9 lb.)

Print Size: 90mm ($3^9/_{16}$") x 140mm ($5^9/_{16}$")

SUPPLIES INCLUDED IN B6 KIT

B6 Printer

Flash Housing

B6 PM, 5/pkg.

Bulbs, 10/pkg.

Ink: 40 cc tubes: Black, Brown, White, Yellow, Green, Blue, Red

Ink Block, 6" x 2"

Blue Filter

Pen, fine point

Card paper, 10 sheets, 4" x 6"

Batteries, 2 AA

Clip Art Sheet

Template Sheet

Instruction booklet

PRINT GOCCO B5

SPECIFICATIONS

Dimensions 310 mm ($12^1/_4$") width x 170 mm ($6^3/_4$") height x 430 mm ($16^{15}/_{16}$") length

Weight 1.3 kg, (2.9 lb.)

Print Size: 150 mm ($3^9/_{16}$") x 220 mm ($8^{11}/_{16}$")

SUPPLIES INCLUDED IN B5 KIT

B5 Printer

Flash Housing

B5 PM, 5/pkg.

Bulbs, 2 pkgs. 10/pkg.

Ink: 40 cc tubes: eight tubes of Black and one tube each of, Brown, White, Yellow, Green, Blue, Red

Cushion Sheet

Ink Block, $6^3/_4$" x 10"

Blue Filter

Pens: Fine, Bold, Chisel

Tube Wringer

Batteries, 3 size C

Clip Art Sheet

Positioning Template

Grid Paper, 10 sheets, 7" x 10"

Instruction booklet

Supply Booklet

GOCCO ACCESSORIES

B6 STAMP KIT FOR CLOTH

B6 Stamper

Ink: Black, Yellow, Blue, Red

Supports: 4

Adhesive Boards: 2, $5^1/_2$" x $8^{15}/_{16}$"

Ink Block, 6" x 2"

Instructions

SCREEN KIT PG KIT

PG 701 Masters, 2/pkg.

PG 702 Masters, 2/pkg.

Textile Ink, 50 cc bottles, Black, Yellow, Blue, Red

B6 Red Filters, 1

2 Plastic Squeegees, 4" and $5^3/_4$"

Correction Fluid, 20 cc

Medium Pen

Ink Knife

Design Booklet

Instructions

GOCCO SUPPLIES

MASTERS, FILTERS, BULBS

B6 Print Masters, 5/ pkg.

B5 Print Masters, 5/ pkg.

PG 701 Masters, 2/ pkg.

PG 702 Masters, 2/ pkg.

B6 Blue Filters, 2/ pkg.

B6 Red Filters, 2/ pkg.

B5 Blue Filters, 2/ pkg.

Bulbs, 10/ pkg.

HIGH MESH INKS, 40 cc tubes

BASIC COLORS

Black, Brown, White, Yellow, Green, Blue, Red

FLUORESCENTS

Pink, Purple (magenta), Green, Orange

METALLICS: PEARLS

Gold, Silver, Bronze, Blue, Green, Red (rose-red)

PASTELS

Pink, Blue, Green, Lavender, Orange

PROCESS INK SET

Cyan (blue), Magenta, Yellow

TRADITIONAL JAPANESE COLORS

Burgundy (Akane), Dark Brown (Karacha), Deep Blue (Konjou), Red Orange (Daidai), Teal (Aotake), Yellow Green (Moegi)

WATER COLOR EFFECTS

Shell Pink, Baby Blue, Apple Green,
Lemon Yellow, Camel Brown, Moon Gray

CLOTH INKS, 40 cc tubes

Black, Brown, White, Yellow, Green, Blue, Red

FELT SHEETS

Felt Sheets: 2 each, white, blue, yellow, pink

Felting Powder

Instructions

PENS, DOUBLE END

.1 mm/.5 mm

.3/.8 mm

Fine/Medium

Medium/Bold

Chisel Straight/Chisel Oblique

Brush Fine/Brush Medium

VIDEOS

Video 1, Introductory

Video 2, Registration, Felt Kit, photos, Cloth Stamper

Video Stamp Kit

MISCELLANEOUS SUPPLIES

Adhesive Boards for Cloth Kit, $8^1/_4''$ x $11^3/_4''$, 10/pkg.

Card Racks, 2/pkg. Hold 20 cards each.

Correction Fluid, 20 cc

Foam Base Pad, B6

Foam Base Pad, B5

Ink Block, 2pcs., 5" x 7"

Ink Cones, 10/pkg.

Master Cleaner, 50 ml

Photo Screen, 65 Line, $3^1/_2''$ x $5^1/_2''$, 2/pkg.

Process Color Design Book
  Japanese instructions, "English" illustrations

Stage Glass B5 (Window)

Stage Glass B6 (Window)

OTHER SUPPLIES

When the creative urge hits, you want to be prepared, supplies on hand, so you can put your energy into your project rather than gathering up items you need. Try to store these near your Printer.

GENERAL SUPPLIES

- As a substitute for Gocco master Cleaner, use Goop, an automotive hand cleaner that will clean High Mesh Ink off Print Masters, fingers, Formica, etc. Don't use it on water-based Stamp Ink for Cloth. Look for Goop in hardware stores and super markets. (There is also an adhesive called Goop. You don't want this one!)

- Simple Green also works for cleaning ink.
- Non-photo blue grid paper, 8 squares per inch. (See REGISTRATION, p.113.)
- Heat gun or toaster oven to melt embossing powder and cure puff paint in fabric printing.
- Tape: masking, scotch, double stick, Tack-A-Note
- Register marks for multi-master printing; Chartpak is one brand.
- Glue stick & repositionable glue stick
- Ring binder note book to save a sample of each project.
- Scissors
- Scrap paper
- Thermography/Embossing powder
- Tracing paper, clear Mylar for registration
- White Out, nail polish or mimeo correction fluid
- X-Acto knife or snap-off blade knife

CREATIVE ACCESSORIES

These are not *essential* to printing, but they certainly are very useful:

- Badge-A-Minit: 345 N. Lewis Ave, Oglesby, IL 61348
- Blank Puzzles: Compoz-A-Puzzle Inc., 7 Littleworth Lane, Sea Cliff, NY 11579, 516-759-1101
- Circle cutter: NT Cutter, C-1500, Nippon Transfer Paper Co., Ltd., Japan.
- Deckle-edge paper cutter
- Paper cutter
- Rubber stamps, glitter, other embellishments
- The Tacker: Fasten all manner of fun things with this fastener gun, (similar to price tags on garments in stores) Think Ink, 7526 Olympic View Dr. Suite E., Edmonds, WA 98026

FABRIC PRINTING INKS

There are many good water-based textile inks for screen printing. Contact your local art store or screen printing supplier for information on specific inks. These are a few suggestions:

- Union Ink Co., 453 Broad Ave., Ridgefield, NJ 07657, 1-800-526-0455. Make a very opaque white-Aerotex white 1020
- Createx, 14 Airport Park Road, East Granby, CT 06026, 1-800-243-2712. They carry white puff paint and luminescent inks in vibrant colors.
- Lumiere, Speedball, and Versatex inks: Good colors, but whites not opaque. Available at many art and craft stores.

MISCELLANEOUS FABRIC PRINTING SUPPLIES

- Disappearing fabric marking pens: wash out or fade-away types
- Squeegees
- Cardboard or foam core board for stabilizing fabric
- Spray glue, e.g., 3-M Spray Adhesive

PAPER SOURCES

Check your Yellow Pages for paper and stationery suppliers. There are many mail order sources.

- Daniel Smith, 4150 First Ave. South, PO Box 84268, Seattle, WA 98124-5568

A good selection of printmaking papers.

WORK AND STORAGE AREA

Printing will be easier if you have a clean, open area to spread out your Printer, supplies and papers. It is also convenient to have one storage place to keep everything ready for when the creative spirit strikes.

GOCCO CARD COMPETITION

Save your creative efforts throughout the year for this annual competition. It is sponsored by the Riso Educational Foundation of Japan, manufactures of Print Gocco. Prizes are certificates, plaques, Gocco products, cash... and that elusive "Fame and Glory!"

- Size: 140 x 150 mm (5 $9/16$" x 5 $15/16$") x 90 x 107 mm (3 $9/16$" x 4 $1/4$")

- Content: holiday cards, greeting cards, invitations, etc.

- Submit 2 copies of each entry to your Gocco dealer.

- Entries must be unpublished Gocco prints or screen print originals

- Deadline: December 31 of every year

ABOUT THE AUTHOR

Claire Russell has worked and experimented with the Gocco Printers since 1981...that's many Print Masters ago! Claire started using the Print Gocco in calligraphy classes she was teaching. The Printer was the carrot rather than the stick approach: practice your letters and see what wonderful projects you can make with this handy little printing machine! Little did she realize what she was getting into!

This book had its genesis in 1982 when Mary Worthington and Claire Russell created a monthly publication, THE GOCCO GAZETTE. This was the beginning not only of the book you are now holding, but a close friendship between the two authors. Mary and Claire realized that there were many underutilized Printers languishing in closets. THE GAZETTE was begun at Mary's suggestion in response to numerous questions from owners of the Print Gocco. After the GAZETTE, the authors decided it was time to compile their information in a book, THE GOCCO GUIDE, published in 1983. The GOCCO GUIDE, however, sparked even more questions and requests for workshops to see "in living color" the techniques they had described. This sent Claire traveling to points far and near teaching a wide range of Gocco techniques.

An expanded version of the GUIDE was the next step. It has been a long time coming. Claire found it was much more work producing a book on her own. "Life" kept getting in the way and delaying the project!

COLOPHON

THE NEW GOCCO GUIDE was begun on a Macintosh SE. Work continued on a Power Macintosh 6100 with Microsoft Word 6.0.1. It was printed on a Hewlett Packard Laser Jet Printer.

Text is in Adobe Optima. Headings are in Neuland.

Printing and binding are by Malloy Lithographing, Inc., Ann Arbor, Michigan, on 70# Glatfelter Thor Offset acid free 85% recycled paper. The soft cover is 12 pt. film laminated.

CREATING WITH PRINT GOCCO
Claire Russell

THE NEW GOCCO GUIDE is a complete resource for ideas and instructions that will answer your Gocco printing questions and fuel your creativity with new ideas.

GENEROUSLY ILLUSTRATED manual has over 200 illustrations and clear, easy to follow instructions. Eighteen chapters cover all aspects of using Gocco Printers including color mixing, fabric printing, projects, and troubleshooting.

LAY FLAT BINDING makes this an easy-to use reference guide, 245 pages, 6" x 9," durable, coated cover.

ORDER NOW

- **THE NEW GOCCO GUIDE** …$29.95
- Shipping, USA …$4.00
- Shipping, airmail worldwide …$8.50
- WA state residents, add $2.92 tax

- THINK INK
  7526 Olympic View Drive, Suite E
  Edmonds, WA 98026-5556

- www.thinkink.net